Decoded

The Science Behind
Why We Buy

Phil Barden

Foreword by Rory Sutherland

WILEY

A John Wiley & Sons, Ltd., Publication

This edition first published 2013
© 2013 John Wiley & Sons
Reprinted with corrections October 2013
Reprinted July 2014
Reprinted February 2015
Registered office
John Wiley & Sons Ltd, The Atrium, Southern Gate, Chichester, West Sussex, PO19 8SQ,
United Kingdom

For details of our global editorial offices, for customer services and for information about how
to apply for permission to reuse the copyright material in this book please see our website at
www.wiley.com.

Wiley publishes in a variety of print and electronic formats and by print-on-demand. Some
material included with standard print versions of this book may not be included in e-books or
in print-on-demand. If this book refers to media such as a CD or DVD that is not included in
the version you purchased, you may download this material at http://booksupport.wiley.com.
For more information about Wiley products, visit www.wiley.com.

Designations used by companies to distinguish their products are often claimed as trademarks.
All brand names and product names used in this book are trade names, service marks,
trademarks or registered trademarks of their respective owners. The publisher is not associated
with any product or vendor mentioned in this book.

Limit of Liability/Disclaimer of Warranty: While the publisher and author have used their best
efforts in preparing this book, they make no representations or warranties with the respect to
the accuracy or completeness of the contents of this book and specifically disclaim any implied
warranties of merchantability or fitness for a particular purpose. It is sold on the
understanding that the publisher is not engaged in rendering professional services and neither
the publisher nor the author shall be liable for damages arising herefrom. If professional
advice or other expert assistance is required, the services of a competent professional should
be sought.

Library of Congress Cataloging-in-Publication Data

[9781118345603]

A catalogue record for this book is available from the British Library.
ISBN 9781118345603 (hardback)   ISBN 9781118345573 (emobi)
ISBN 9781118345580 (epdf)   ISBN 9781118345597 (epub)

Cover design: Jason Anscomb

Set in Sabon Std 10.5/16 pt by Toppan Best-set Premedia Limited
Printed in Italy by Printer Trento

For Luke and Jack

Contents

Foreword

If it seems strange to open the foreword to a book about marketing by making reference to a 16th-century Danish astronomer, please do bear with me for a moment.

Tycho Brahe (1546–1601) is now credited by many historians of science as being the man who made the work of Kepler and Newton possible.

The formulation of the laws of physics which have proved so useful in the physical sciences was possible only because of Brahe's work in cataloguing the movements of celestial bodies. Without the hoard of empirical data amassed by Brahe, the theories propounded by his student Kepler or by Newton may never have come about. Or – equally likely – other theories may have appeared and persisted which were plausible and expedient, but simply wrong.

Quite a few people, among them the economist Paul Ormerod, have used this point to make a fairly damning attack on conventional economic theory. And with good reason. The theory of human action advanced by neo-classical economics is not founded on any empirical observation of how people make decisions, or on any research into neuroscience: instead, unlike the advances in astronomy and physics, where observation led to theory, the process was made to work the other way round: a plausible theory was developed of how human beings should make economic decisions, and a whole body of work was then constructed by extrapolation from these initial assumptions.

But these assumptions, though convenient, may turn out to be almost entirely wrong. People do not make decisions based on perfect information; they do not compare value between different categories; and they are not unaffected by the behaviour of other people (or by their own past behaviour) when making their decisions. Nor are their preferences or ideas of value unaffected by context. Once you acknowledge these truths, the whole mathematical edifice of economic thought starts to crack at the foundations.

But a similar accusation could be levelled at the (considerably feebler) school of thought that drives most marketing decision making. Marketing seldom attempts to be much of a science in any case, but, when it does, it certainly does not attempt to be an empirical science. Again, like economics, it takes an assumption on how people should be influenced in any course of action and then constructs a whole set of 'rules' derived from that initial assumption. It also decides its actions on the basis of a spectacularly dangerous delusion: that people know and can accurately describe the mental mechanisms underlying their decisions and actions.

What Phil has done with this book is to fire a powerful and timely salvo in the battle against this backwards approach.

So, while this is ostensibly a book about marketing, it has implications for fields far beyond it. The book collates a large body of scientific evidence which shows that people do not make decisions in the way marketers (or economists) commonly and simplistically assume. So, just as economics has often been blind to a wide range of human emotions and tendencies (such as regret, loss aversion, contagion or the endowment effect), it seems that marketers have been similarly blind to a whole range of unconscious influences on human decision making (such as context, goal dilution, path dependency or framing).

For this reason, the book – and its wealth of case studies and citations – is invaluable to marketers and to anyone working in an ad agency, in a digital agency, in market research or in media. But it is also of importance to anyone who seeks to understand people, their perceptions and their motivations: politicians, policy makers, retailers, product designers, financial regulators, legislators and businesses of every kind.

And I very much hope these other people discover the book. For I rather suspect it may gain more traction there than within the marketing and advertising community. Why? Because, to be frank, the record of the marketing services community to what seems to be a Copernican revolution in the behavioural sciences has so far been mostly notable by its absence. The past reaction to earlier work by Ehrenberg, Jones, Stephen King and so on – which challenges assumptions with real empirical evidence – suggests that marketers may do what they usually do: show great interest and appreciation of this new information, before carrying on doing what they have always done. 'Yes, all very good, Phil, but I'm behind target for the month on my Facebook "Likes".'

Or, as Upton Sinclair observed long before the concept of 'loss aversion' had been scientifically observed: 'It is difficult to get a man to understand something when his salary depends upon his not understanding it.'

But let's not despair quite yet. First of all this book is unusual in that it is not only a very useful collection of observations, it also explains what we should do in response. It is more than just a new way of looking at the marketing universe, valuable though that is: it is also an eminently practical handbook which tells you what to do differently in response.

And it is also very timely. Earlier marketers, among them David Ogilvy, Bill Bernbach and Howard Gossage, have striven for a more intelligent approach to understanding human behaviour (Gossage even founded a company called Generalists, Inc, which was an attempt in the 1960s to connect marketing to the behavioural sciences). And all good direct marketers – including my first boss, the wonderful Drayton Bird – have been first-rate behavioural psychologists. Deep down, everyone good in marketing has known instinctively for years that marketing has a vast and disabling blind spot in understanding both individual and collective behaviour.

The problem everyone faced back then was that, without the vocabulary and the overarching body of theory, talking about this stuff made you seem trivial and small-minded. No one got promoted for changing the choices on a coupon, even though that might have had a bigger effect on sales and profits than long, self-aggrandizing hours spent discussing the typography of the TV commercial's endframe. #OgilvyChange even has a mantra to underscore the importance of these small things: 'Dare to be Trivial.'

But now, finally, we have a vocabulary to match the importance of these findings. I am no longer 'just designing the coupon', I am a 'choice architect'. Finally those areas of marketing activity which were typically delegated to the office boy may start to find their place in the marketing director's office, or even the boardroom.

This new vocabulary is, of course, a wonderful example of 'reframing' at work.

How elegant is that?

Rory Sutherland
Executive Creative Director and Vice-Chairman, OgilvyOne London
and Vice-Chairman, Ogilvy Group UK

Preface

I spent 25 years of my life in Unilever, Diageo and T-Mobile trying to influence consumer behaviour in favour of my brands and products. In order to achieve this, we as marketers accumulate a huge amount of information and sophisticated analyses about our customers. Indeed, companies such as those for which I worked have developed models and processes that capture years of collective experience. These models guide our multi-million investments in product development and innovation, communication and research. However, the true reasons why we, as human beings, do what we do remain a mystery. Otherwise the failure rate of new products would be nowhere near the reported 80–90 per cent and advertising budgets would be totally efficient and effective.

But marketing life's not like that. Sometimes my activities were successful, sometimes they were not, and based on my personal experience, and in common with many marketers, I built my own mental model of how consumers decide. I knew that this belief system was far from perfect, but no one had a better one to offer – each had his own belief system, which of course led to massive internal discussions (or arguments!), ending in decisions based on personal preferences, often dictated by hierarchy.

This is symptomatic of a more general point, and one that should concern all marketers – a recent study by the Fournaise Marketing Group among 1,200 CEOs across North America, Europe and Asia Pacific reported that 80 per cent of chief executives believe marketers are 'disconnected' from business results and focus on the wrong areas. More specifically, 78 per cent of respondents said that marketers 'too often lose sight of what their real job is' – namely, to increase demand for goods and services in a quantifiable way. The research concluded that marketers will have to transform themselves into true return on investment (ROI)-driven business people if they are to earn the trust of CEOs and if they want to have a bigger impact in the boardroom. Otherwise they will forever remain in what 65 per cent of CEOs call 'marketing la-la land'.

A sobering challenge indeed, yet marketers hold the key to company revenue – understanding consumers, and translating that into compelling product and service propositions. As brand custodians we've always known that brands have some sort of intangible quality over and above the pure functionality of whatever product or service they grace. This is what we've called brand 'equity', but it's always been difficult to pin down, explain and make tangible. No wonder CEOs think marketing's 'fluffy' and trust their CFOs more than their CMOs. To step out of la-la land and earn that trust we must make brand equity tangible and understandable and explain better why it's by no means trivial. It's what enables brands to command a price premium compared with more commodity-like alternatives. Consumers are willing to pay £2 or £3 for a coffee in Starbucks, yet they know, objectively, that for the price of two cups they could buy a whole jar of coffee in a supermarket. So they must be buying something else. Some sort of value applies over and above the physical product, but what is it? How does the brain perceive such value? In short, how do consumers decide?

Whenever science enters a domain it adds significant value, but, ironically, the mental model we apply in marketing today is still based on 1970s' thinking – almost half a century ago! In this time, the understanding in the areas of decision science has advanced dramatically. It behoves us to update the way we think about how consumers decide. From my perspective, the knee-jerk reaction of the marketing community in the last few years has been to delegate this scientific evolution to their market researchers, utilizing new ways of measurement like brain scanning. But do we really think that we need even more data? And what if such new methodologies generate similar results – a likely outcome since most of them are validated using existing models and metrics? Or what if they show differences? What then is right and what is wrong, and how should we make this judgement? As long as we continue to ask the same questions and don't update our mental model for consumer decision making, we will not be able to exploit the powerful insights that decision science offers. This requires a paradigm shift in marketing, not just a change of tools.

So why have I written this book? Because my belief system was significantly shaken four years ago. I was then Vice-President Brand Development for T-Mobile, taking the brand through changes in brand architecture and positioning. I was confronted by a totally new mental model for marketing and consumer decision making based on decision science: the conclusions from the latest collective learnings from neuroscience, behavioural economics, cognitive and social psychology. I found it fascinating because it offered me explanations of consumer behaviour which previously had mystified me, but at the same time it was irritating because it disproved some of my very basic assumptions about how consumers decide. It was the first time I had experienced the power of an approach that was based not on beliefs and assumptions but on the latest scientific findings. Using this knowledge not only yielded new vocabulary that was more valuable in understanding why consumers do what they do but at the same time provided a profound framework for marketing – from brand strategy and positioning, through to innovation, advertising and interactive media.

This approach was not only fascinating and different, it proved to be a huge financial success for the brand, inspiring the 'Dance' advertising campaign in the UK. In a fiercely competitive market, the results were stunning:

- 146 per cent ROI
- sales increased by 49 per cent
- market share grew by 6 per cent
- customer acquisition costs halved
- brand consideration tripled
- retail store footfall doubled and conversion grew by 20 per cent
- existing customers increased their usage of the services, spending 11 per cent more than the market
- 36 million YouTube views, 68 Facebook groups.

(Source: T-Mobile and IPA)

Consequentially, this approach has been applied across all other T-mobile brand 'touch points', such as proposition development, retail store design and customer services. According to Lysa Hardy, until recently the T-Mobile VP in the UK, the combined effect of these changes, and subsequent advertising based on the same communications platform, is that T-Mobile has halved its customer churn (the percentage of customers who leave the network). From being the worst churn in the UK mobile network market three years ago, it is now the best and is at an all-time low. The approach has subsequently been rolled out by the brand across Europe, resulting in further industry recognition for its achievements, including an award for the best brand relaunch.

Inspired by this, I started to dive deep into the literature of decision science. As I suspected, the mental model I had applied for all those years was far from complete – and, in many cases, simply wrong. I became more and more fascinated by what I learned and its value in building brands and driving revenue. This experience was so profound and exciting that it inspired me to switch careers. I left my job at T-Mobile and joined

Decode, the consultancy responsible for the step change I had experienced at T-Mobile, and they have kept me on a steep learning curve for the past three years.

Decode was founded, and is staffed, by former scientists from the fields of decision science. To stay at the leading edge of developments, Decode collaborates with leading universities for neuro-economics, such as the California Institute of Technology (USA). In addition, its consultants still practise, at professorial and doctoral level, in academe. They have been complemented by practitioners from advertising and brand management to form an interdisciplinary team of experts with a unique blend of capabilities, translating the latest scientific learnings into pragmatic and concrete marketing application. This bridge from science to day-to-day marketing practice is what this book is about.

The goal of this book is to share what I learned on my journey about bringing decision science to life for marketing, and the fascinating insights I have come across about why consumers buy what they buy. We now have a framework, a language and a growing body of knowledge to enable marketers to address the real drivers of brand choice. Most importantly, with this book I want to empower the reader to harness this valuable knowledge and apply it to everyday marketing work. The benefits of doing so resonate with my personal experience and are echoed consistently by feedback we receive from clients and their agencies: better explanatory and predictive power from a new and deeper level of insight, sharper propositions, more precise briefings, greater efficiency and effectiveness in the client–agency relationship, more confidence and an enhanced ability to scale knowledge and training. Additionally, multinational clients have enjoyed a release from the tension and frustration involved in typical 'centre' versus 'local' debates about brand positioning and creative development. Last, and by no means least, decision science offers a way for marketers to step into the boardroom and leave la-la land behind.

I hope you enjoy this journey as much as I have.

Author's note: There are many studies and experiments cited in this book. These are referenced in a section at the end. More details about these, and other topics related to the book, can be found at www.decoded-book.com.

1
Decision Science

Understanding the Why of Consumer Behaviour

In marketing our goal is to influence purchase decisions. But what drives those decisions? Decision sciences help to answer this crucial question by uncovering the underlying mechanisms, rules and principles of decision making. These fascinating and valuable insights from science have been expanding rapidly in the past few years. This chapter will go into some of the depths of the latest learnings from decision science, but don't worry, you don't need to be a scientist to swim here! We will see what really drives purchasing behaviour, and how to apply these insights to maximize the benefit to marketing. Most importantly, we will introduce a practical framework to harness the learnings in our everyday marketing roles.

Let there be light!

No advert in recent times has won more prizes for creativity or received more public and media attention than Cadbury's 'Gorilla'. Brand volumes had been fairly static for years and the brand had suffered the effects of a significant quality problem the previous year. So Cadbury's objective was to get back into the British public's 'hearts and minds' with a new advert. The agency's brief was to 'rediscover the joy'. This resulted in the 'Gorilla' advert, in which a gorilla first anticipates and then starts drumming along to the Phil Collins song 'In the air tonight'. The advert achieved huge amounts of interest and attention, not only from consumers but also from those of us working in brand management. It was a very unusual ad for the category, not least with a gorilla as opposed to the chocolate product taking centre stage. The advert (Figure 1.1) does not contain the usual food or consumption shots either and only at the very end is the packaging shown.

Spurred on by the hype and excitement caused by 'Gorilla', Cadbury immediately ordered a follow-up campaign. You'd think that nothing could be simpler, yet despite a similar strategy, the same brief, same agency, same director, same campaign objective and media budget, the sequel did not meet client expectations at all. How can this be? Why was 'Gorilla' successful in the client's eyes but the sequel clearly failed? We've all experienced similar situations with our own work. Some ads take off and are

Figure 1.1 The much talked about Cadbury 'Gorilla' TV advertisement

long-running successes, others fail – and, more often than not, it is hard, if not impossible, to decode the underlying reasons for success and failure.

Another area where the key success principles are often unclear is innovation and new product development. As we all know, the majority of new products launched in any one year fail. Which of us hasn't experienced cases where our product launches were failures despite market research giving them the green light? Research is carried out, tests are run and, in the end, the predictions are simply wrong. Not only is this costly to the enterprise in terms of wasted resources, it's also intensely frustrating for us marketers due to the unanswered questions that subsequently plague us: What did we overlook? What went wrong? And what can we learn from this in order to prevent us from simply following a trial-and-error approach? What can we improve in our thinking and process? The uncertainty dangles like the sword of Damocles over the heads of those people responsible and their colleagues, which is not exactly conducive for the next innovation.

The reverse scenario happens, too: an innovation, which might actually have been successful, isn't even introduced because market research predicted it would fail. To give an example, Baileys liqueur was rejected by consumers but was launched anyway and turned out to be a great success. Likewise, during product testing prior to Red Bull's introduction, customer comments like 'yuk', 'disgusting', 'tastes like medicine' and 'I would never drink this' were commonplace, and yet today Red Bull is available almost everywhere in the world and is hugely successful.

In times of reduced budgets and a growing requirement to justify marketing expenditure, achieving effective branding in our activities is crucial. This is not only a critical factor in our return on investment, it also ensures that we don't spend money to benefit the competition or, indeed, solely advertise to support the whole category. Our communication should anchor our brands efficiently in the minds of consumers. If 'branding' scores are below the required benchmark in a pre-test, how often have we heard (or even made) recommendations such as 'make the logo bigger'? However, it is unlikely that these kinds of recommendations will fix the problem. When we look at the image in Figure 1.2, what brand is it for?

We can immediately recognize it as O2 – even without any direct brand information like the logo. But how do we know? One could argue that the bubbles are a key visual for the brand. This is true, but does this mean that any kind of bubble would activate the O2 brand? Probably not, so what is it that makes it O2? What are the principles that underlie successful branding? While some ads achieve above-average brand recall, for others the brand linkage is very weak – and yet our brand logo is always integrated somehow, so why exactly do these differences occur?

Despite all our efforts, be it working on strategy, communication or market research, the direct path to successful marketing often resembles a stumble through a weakly illuminated black box, and still leaves many questions unanswered.

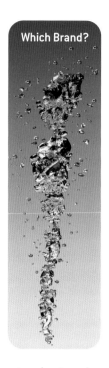

Figure 1.2 The brand isn't present and yet we know it

If these examples ring any bells then they help illustrate that, in order to make progress, we need to better understand how people really decide, and what drives their decisions when it comes to choosing brands and products. The great news is that there is now a systematic approach to human decision making that we can take, one that is both scientifically valid and practical for marketers.

Decision science and economics merge

In a study into the neural bases of decision making, German neuro-economist Professor Peter Kenning and his associates looked at brain scans of people who had been shown photographs of pairs of brands. These photos either included the person's stated favourite brand or did not. Every time they were shown one of the photographs, each person was told to choose a brand to buy. There were two main findings. First, when the favourite brand was included, the brain areas activated were different to when two non-favourite brands were exposed. When the favourite brand was present, the choice was made instantly and, correspondingly, the brain showed significantly less activity in areas involved in reflective thinking, an effect the scientists named 'cortical relief'. Instead, brain regions involved in intuitive decision making were activated (in particular the so-called ventro-medial prefrontal cortex in the frontal lobe). In other words, strong brands have a real effect in the brain, and this effect is to enable intuitive and rapid decision making without thinking.

Second, this cortical relief effect occurs only for the respondent's number one brand – even the brand ranked second does not trigger this intuitive decision making. The scientists call this the 'first-choice brand effect'. One target we set as marketers is to be in our target consumer's relevant, or consideration, set. This research indicates that the optimal target is to maximize the number of consumers for whom we are the number one brand – being in the relevant set is not sufficient to enable this intuitive decision making and, of course, no revenue is earned by the brand that was nearly bought!

Intuitive decision making, as a process, is what enables a shopper to stand in front of a shelf and make purchase decisions in milliseconds. But it's not only about brand and product purchases; it is a characteristic of our everyday lives. It's even relevant when it comes to numerical logic. In the introduction to his acceptance speech for the Nobel Prize, psychologist Daniel Kahneman posed the following simple question:

A baseball bat and a ball cost $1.10 together. The bat costs $1 more than the ball. How much does the ball cost?

It's simple, isn't it? Nearly everyone to whom this question is posed imme-diately and intuitively answers that the ball costs 10 cents. This intuitive response was also true of the majority of students at the elite universities of Princeton and Harvard, among whom this exercise was originally con-ducted. Nearly everyone gives this answer. But it's incorrect. The ball actually costs only 5 cents (reason: $1.05 for the bat plus $0.05 for the ball equals $1.10). Something in our brain leads most of us, intuitively, to give an incorrect answer to this apparently simple calculation. Instead of doing the mathematics, we resort to our gut feel that, given the $1 price of the bat, 10 cents feels about right as the price for the ball. This intui-tion is based on the ease of perceiving the split of the 1.10 price tag into two chunks of $1 and 10 cents respectively. Doing the actual calculation is much harder for our brain, and most of us don't bother because the 10 cent answer feels just right.

Using examples like these, Daniel Kahneman investigates how decisions are influenced through psychological processes. By bridging psychology and economics, Kahneman's work results in a major opportunity to sys-tematically integrate the psychological world with the world of economics and, in so doing, to exploit the full explanatory power of consumer deci-sion making that the combination of both approaches provides.

Economics and psychology were, for a very long time, two completely separate worlds. Economists start with the basic idea of a rational human being who makes decisions according to objective cost versus utility analy-ses. Psychologists, meanwhile, emphasize the psychological character of decision making, where the evaluation of value and utility appear irra-tional, following a kind of psycho-logic. Nowadays, if you do a Google search for 'neuro-economics', neuro-marketing' or 'behavioural econom-ics', you will find millions of returns. Among the major drivers of this change were the insights of Daniel Kahneman, the first psychologist to receive the Nobel Prize in Economic Sciences in 2002.

A science-based framework for marketing

Literally thousands of research papers are being published every year in academic journals such as the *Journal of Neuroscience*, *Journal of Consumer Psychology*, *Journal of Experimental Psychology* and *Behaviour and Brain Sciences*. There are so many studies and so much data coming from these new fields of decision science, but how can we make sense of them all and integrate the resultant understanding with what we do in marketing?

To translate and transfer the insights to our marketing world we need a framework that allows us to systematically apply the most important principles, rules and mechanisms offered by science. The framework we will use to structure this knowledge is also provided by science and is that which Kahneman introduced (see Figure 1.3), and for which he was rewarded with the Nobel Prize. It represents the summary and culmination of the key findings from his life's work on human decision making. Since

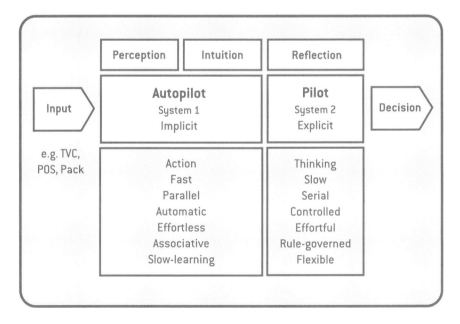

Figure 1.3 Illustration of Kahneman's Nobel Prize-winning framework showing the two systems that determine our decisions and behaviour

the award, Kahneman's model has been supported by many subsequent studies, including many from the neurosciences, which have also further validated and extended his view of decision making. In his 2011 bestselling book *Thinking, Fast and Slow*, Kahneman gives an up-to-date review of the science underlying his framework.

The core of Kahneman's framework is the distinction between two systems of mental processes that determine our decisions and behaviour. He calls these two systems 'System 1' and 'System 2'. System 1 integrates perception and intuition. It's always running – Kahneman says that it 'never sleeps'. It's very fast, processes all information in parallel, and is effortless, associative and slow-learning. It is made for fast, automatic, intuitive actions without thinking. Automaticity is crucial because it's efficient and hence consumes less energy. In times when energy was a scarce resource this efficient way of acting and deciding was key to survival. Reflective thinking requires energy so, in a way, our brain is not made for thinking, but for fast and automated actions. The most highly skilled mental activities are based on System 1, such as cardiologists interpreting an ECG trace, chess masters deciding on the next move, or agency creatives coming up with a new design. In contrast, system 2 is slow, works step by step, takes up a lot of energy because it is effortful, but has the benefit of being flexible. It enables us to make reflective, deliberate decisions. It is made for thinking.

The experiment cited earlier that revealed that brands induce 'cortical relief' shows that strong brands are processed in System 1. Indeed, the hallmark of a strong brand is to activate System 1 and circumvent System 2 processing. Weak brands, by contrast, activate System 2, i.e. consumers have to think about the purchase decision.

Subjectively we do not usually experience that there are two separate systems at work and, in the end, we make one coherent decision. We notice both systems only when they are in conflict, as in the baseball bat example above. We reflectively understand the calculation but our intuition just tells us something different. Another demonstration of the same principle is shown

yellow	**yellow**	**blue**	blue	yellow
green	**green**	green	red	**yellow**
green	white	**yellow**	**blue**	**red**
black	red	red	yellow	blue
red	blue	**red**	**green**	red

Figure 1.4 The Stroop test demonstrates the two systems in action

by the following exercise. Have a look through the table in Figure 1.4 column by column and say out loud as quickly as possible the *colours of the words* (i.e. you start at the top left corner with 'green', 'black', 'red' ...).

You didn't find it that easy, did you? At the very least it took you considerable effort and concentration. The meaning of each word can be automatically processed, as can the colour (System 1). However, when word meaning and colour are in conflict, naming the colour takes some time and needs to be done reflectively (System 2). The two pieces of information do not match and this induces a conflict, leading to us requiring more control and concentration to avoid mistakes. As you progressed through the exercise, known as the Stroop test, you probably found it increasingly demanding, requiring you to concentrate harder in order not to make a mistake. This is because the more effortful System 2 is tiring the brain and so it reverts to the more energy-efficient System 1. This exercise also shows the ubiquity of System 1 – it's present in everything we do, including reading and speaking our mother tongue.

A useful metaphor for how the two systems work together is to see System 1 as an autopilot and System 2 as a pilot. The pilot is responsible for tasks that require flexible decision making, such as take-off and landing or when a problem occurs, whereas the autopilot is responsible for all the decisions that can be made automatically. As long as there are no problems, the pilot relies on the processing of the autopilot for the entire flight without really knowing what is going on in the autopilot. None of the workings of the autopilot are transparent to the pilot. The autopilot works implicitly whereas the decisions of the pilot are explicit. To get a deeper insight into the nature of these systems let's look at something we've all experienced: driving a car.

As we saw in the illustration of Kahneman's framework, the autopilot is connected to what we perceive through all our senses. In terms of our first driving lesson, the assault on our senses was a nightmare. We had to concentrate on the traffic signals, steer, indicate and brake all at the same time, as well as listening to our driving instructor's advice and directions. The resulting problems with hand–eye coordination, decoding the traffic signals and generally dealing with a lot of incoming data typically led to a sense of overwhelming panic. We had to think a lot, so this made us slow to respond and react. Our decisions were dominated by the pilot system, because we were not able to base them on intuition since intuition is based on experience. But it got better with practice and the need to concentrate reduced. We now know where third gear is without having to look at the gear shift. When we think of how we drive to work, all of these things that once appeared so stressful and overwhelming now simply happen intuitively. We navigate through traffic, we stop at red without really focusing on the traffic lights, and we complete all of these complex tasks while listening to music or even making phone calls (hands free, of course). And sometimes we wonder how we even got from A to B because we did not pay conscious attention to our driving throughout the entire journey.

We do all of this automatically and intuitively. When we learn something for the first time, the pilot is engaged. Then, with repetition and based on the experience, we develop intuition and the processes become automated and, consequently, more efficient. We become driving experts. The underlying learning process is the same in general, for doctors, chess masters, agency creatives and even consumers since they have a lot of experience of seeing advertising and of buying and using the products.

Once we have sufficient experience under our belts, and have developed our intuition, the pilot system comes into play only when we face new problems or something we have not experienced before. If, on our way to work, the road we normally use is closed due to roadworks, we suddenly have to think what detour to take. In this situation we most probably turn down the radio or end our phone conversation because we need to concentrate.

On the one hand, we have a strong tendency for automation in our brain and on the other we have the benefit of deliberation and reflective thinking in order to solve new problems. These are the hallmarks of why these systems have evolved.

There are two decision-making systems at work in any decision we make: an implicit system working like an autopilot, and an explicit system operating like a pilot.

So there are two systems operating in our brains – this is a general characteristic of decision making. For marketers, it's crucial to understand these two systems, as they determine purchase decisions across all categories, industries, brands and products. So let's look further at how the autopilot and the pilot work.

The (almost) unlimited capacity of the autopilot

Think of a typical kitchen area at your office. Next to the kettle, there might be a box in which to make a monetary contribution towards the cost of buying tea, coffee and milk. This is known as an 'honesty box'. Generally, there's a gap between the cost of tea, coffee and milk that is

Figure 1.5 The autopilot processes signals in the environment even if we are not consciously aware of them

consumed and how much money is contributed. An experiment showed that when a cut-out pair of eyes was positioned close to the box (see Figure 1.5), people were significantly more inclined to pay for their consumption. The employees did not generally notice the eyes as they were focusing on making coffee or tea. But the pair of eyes must have been processed by the autopilot system because this significantly influenced behaviour. The eyes implicitly activated the same social norms that would be followed if someone else were in the room. Without employees noticing the impact of this, it nevertheless led to more honest behaviour.

What this experiment shows is that the autopilot processes a huge range of information, not only that on which we focus but also all the contextual information in the environment. When we are in front of a shelf in the supermarket, our autopilot therefore processes much more than just the product on which we are currently focusing: other products on the shelf, the shelf layout, colours, interior design, odours, light levels in the store, music and much more. Similarly, when we visit a website, our autopilot processes the page layout, colours, design and content over and above that which we're looking at.

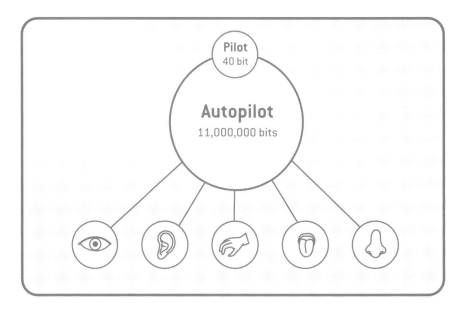

Figure 1.6 The enormous capacity of the autopilot processes everything we experience through our senses

The autopilot processes every single bit of information that is perceived by our senses. It has a huge processing capacity of 11 million bits per second, roughly the size of an old floppy disk (1.4 megabytes) (see Figure 1.6). Each second our senses deliver 11 million bits to the autopilot – no matter whether we're aware of this input or not. And every input is processed by the autopilot and can potentially influence our behaviour. One study shows that when we visit websites the autopilot will derive a first impression within less than one second – and this impression strongly influences our subsequent behaviour.

Comparing this with the very limited capacity of the pilot system, the superiority of the autopilot becomes obvious. A classic finding in cognitive psychology is that the upper limit of our working memory, which is the basis for the pilot to do its thinking, is 7 +/–2 chunks of information (e.g. numbers, letters, words or faces), which amounts to roughly 40–50 bits in the case of numbers or letters. This limited capacity of the pilot is the reason why we find it difficult to remember phone numbers that exceed seven digits. It is also the reason why it is so hard to follow a presentation when someone is whispering next to us, a phone rings or someone leaves the room. We are distracted, we are not able to follow what's being said and we miss some of the information. Likewise, if you think about all of the decisions we make before we leave for work in the morning, 40 bits is not enough to get us out of the house! If we were to reflectively think about every purchase decision in the supermarket, it would take so long to do our shopping that we would starve to death. Even if we wanted to decide reflectively, our very limited capacity constrains us from doing so.

What's more, the typical duration of an average contact with advertising media also shows that most processing does not involve the slow pilot system:

- advert in popular magazines: 1.7 seconds
- advertising in trade journals (e.g. *The Lancet*): 3.2 seconds
- poster: 1.5 seconds
- mailing (first relevance check): 2 seconds
- banner ad: 1 second.

This makes it clear that most marketing communications need to deliver their core messages within seconds. Given the time that would be required to reflectively process all the information in an advertisement, it is obvious that very little of this will be processed by the slow pilot system. Therefore the autopilot, with its high bandwidth and its ability to process information very rapidly, provides marketers with the opportunity to convey messages in a minimal time span.

Suggestion

Read the text of one of your adverts or brochures and note the time it takes you to do this. How long does the customer need to read and digest everything?

The high capacity of the autopilot is also what enables us to include the context within which a decision is made when we actually make that decision. The autopilot processes everything that is perceivable in the environment at any given moment in time, even without focused attention. We've all experienced the power of the autopilot in action without our focused attention in the so-called 'cocktail party effect'. While fully engaged in conversation at a loud party, we nevertheless immediately notice if someone around us mentions our name. This phenomenon occurs only because our autopilot is constantly processing everything, no matter whether we are focusing on the information or not. So if we manage to use this high bandwidth efficiently in our marketing communications, then our messages can have significantly more impact.

The autopilot processes almost every signal in the environment due to its enormous capacity. Therefore even peripheral, subtle signals in the environment can influence decision making and behaviour.

What fires together wires together

What does the brain, or more specifically the autopilot, do with all the input it receives? It's used for learning. But the way the autopilot learns is different to what we normally think of when we think of learning. This learning is not like the way we learn in school, rather it is based on what is called associative learning. Let's look at an example.

The first time we hear the word 'No' it is just a phonetic pattern, a sound. But we recognize that the voice becomes louder and Mum's face looks different the second time she says it. Some minutes later the word 'No' is accompanied by her taking something away from us. After a while we learn the meaning of the word 'No'. This implicit learning is completely different to how we learn a foreign language in school. If we are walking down the street with our mother and there is a group of rough-looking youths in front of us, we experience our mother holding our hand more tightly and she starts to distance us from them, and perhaps walks quicker. The next day she acts similarly, but this time not because of a gang of youths but because of a dog. This time she says, 'Watch out for the dog, it might bite you.' What we learn is that when there is some danger, our hand is held more tightly. And consequently, we learn that the youths are also associated with danger, because then we experienced the same behaviour pattern. Later, when we see a TV ad where a hand is held tighter, and after the brand appears the grip on the hand is released, we directly understand that there was a danger that was resolved by this brand and so we build a learned association between the brand or product and 'safety'.

The principle underlying all of this associative learning is: 'What fires together wires together.' Neuropsychology shows that our brain builds associative connections between signals when they appear at the same time or space and when this simultaneous appearance happens repeatedly over time. If something happens to us once it's probably a random occurrence, but if the same thing happens regularly then our brain starts to learn it, as it has a higher probability of occurring again. Neural cells, which repeatedly fire together, get wired together more and more tightly.

Before we are born, our brain's associative network and our memory can be compared to a field covered with fresh snow. Gaining experiences and learning new things is like walking across the field, leaving fresh footprints in the snow. After some time, the paths that have been well trodden (because we have repeatedly experienced similar things) become fast and easier to navigate, whereas those that have been walked only once or seldom are less well defined and therefore are less likely to be used. So if we smell freshly brewed coffee and a few minutes later the family gathers together in the same room and we experience this several times, a link is created between this smell and the concept of 'companionship'. If we see our father making a cup of coffee when he has to work we build the association of 'work' with coffee. So when we grow up it just feels natural, and intuitive, to drink coffee at work. We might also see someone drinking coffee in the pub, but since this is an exception, the link between coffee and occasions associated with a pub will remain very weak.

The brain does not store information individually like a computer, but instead organizes the world into so-called neural networks where everything is interconnected, which is why this type of memory is also called 'associative memory'. So when we think of coffee, not only is companionship activated but so is everything else that is associated with companionship (e.g. a cake). If we repeatedly see a certain visual representation of bubbles accompanied by the O2 branding, then we implicitly learn the connection between the specific characteristics of the typical O2 bubbles and the brand.

The autopilot needs about 10,000 hours' experience of a specific topic before intuition develops fully. It is not sufficient to see our father make a cup of coffee once while at work. Rather, we need to experience this very often for the autopilot to establish a strong connection between work and coffee. Once established, this intuitive knowledge enables rapid decision making. Experienced cardiologists simply have a look at an ECG to see the relevant patterns. They just know what to do intuitively. But this intuition is far from being a feeling in the way the term 'gut feeling' might indicate. The gut feeling of experts is really implicit knowledge. Consumers are experts as well – in buying and consuming products, brands and communication. Their autopilots have spent much more than 10,000 hours in consuming products and brands, making purchase decisions and being exposed to advertising all day long.

But even experts – professionals or consumers – do not have access to their implicit knowledge. Asked why or how they do what they do, consumers often refer to their gut feeling ('It just feels right'), which is the only conscious signal we get from the autopilot. Unfortunately, the terms 'well-being' or 'feel good' are part of many brand positioning statements and briefings, although they are not themselves the drivers of the decision but generic indicators. It's our only consciously accessible signal of the processes taking place in our implicit system. Kahneman's framework and the underlying science help, as we will see in this book, to make this implicit level of knowledge both tangible and manageable.

Implicit associative learning enables us to efficiently and automatically make sense of the signals we perceive.

Framing – the autopilot frames our experience

So there are two systems operating in our brains – but at the end of the day we have to derive a decision about which product or brand to buy. How does this work? How do the autopilot and pilot interact when we buy? Let's look at an example.

A cosmetic company wanted to develop a new skin cream, so they conducted tests where they made consumers use the different formulas, unbranded, to see which formula was superior. They conducted this research in several cities. When looking at the results they found that in one city one of the creams scored much better than in the other cities. However, all the other creams tested in that particular city did not show the city to be a general factor. After much investigation they discovered the reason for the effect: in that specific city a different jar was used because the standard jar was not available. The replacement jar, however, differed in shape. And it was this seemingly trivial difference that significantly altered the participants' evaluation of the cream. The jar framed how the cream and its performance were perceived. The reason for this is that the autopilot in our head processes even the most subtle signals (such as the shape of a jar) and this in turn can colour the overall product experience.

Every perceivable signal can frame our decisions. In an experiment on scent, people entering a shopping mall were exposed to different kinds of aromas, such as baking cookies or roasting coffee beans. On their way through the mall they encountered someone who, unbeknown to them, was involved in the experiment. This person pretended that they needed some help, for example in selecting something to buy or picking up items when they'd dropped their bag. The people who had been exposed to the aroma of baking cookies were more likely to help than those who hadn't. Again the test subjects were not specifically aware of the scent when they entered the mall, but this signal influenced their behaviour.

It's not only signals from the outside world but also our own internal states that change our choices, decisions and behaviour as well. We know that when we're in a good mood, we can easily look beyond the mistakes of our work colleagues; our good mood directly flows into our decisions, it radiates. We come up with different ideas when we're in a typical work-space than those we generate on a terrace overlooking the ocean – spatial conditions also work on us in the background. In workshops, it can even help us to come up with new ideas if we merely change places with someone. The background indirectly affects everything that we do without us being aware of it.

How does this work? What is the principle that underlies these effects? Figure 1.7 shows a key illustration from Kahneman's Nobel Prize speech. At first one wonders why he uses such an old trick of perception in what is probably the most important speech of his career as a scientist. This is not about the illusion of perception itself, however, but about what may be the most basic principle in our brain. The image shows what scientists call the framing effect. Framing is a key concept in understanding how decisions are made. Understanding this principle leads to a comprehension of how the autopilot and pilot come up with an integrated purchase decision together.

If we look at the two small squares in the centre, it seems as if they are lying in front of the larger ones. The small squares are in the so-called

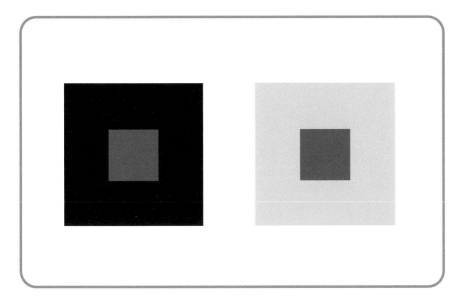

Figure 1.7 Framing: the background changes the perception of the grey square in the foreground

foreground; they are what scientists call the figure. The large squares form the so-called background, they frame the little squares. The two grey squares in the centre appear to have different shades of grey colour. But they don't. Objectively, both grey squares are identical, but subjectively there is a clear difference. The perception of different shades of colour of the two centre squares (the figure) are created only by the different shades of colour of the large squares in the background. The background frames and, with that, changes perception. This means that the background 'radiates' onto the figure and changes its appearance.

The jar was the background influencing the perception of the cream. Customers, of course, focused on the cream because that was what they wanted to evaluate, but the background framed the perception of the cream. The scent of coffee framed the perception of the experience in the mall and thereby influenced behaviour. This framing happens implicitly. We are not aware of the influence, we do not even notice this effect and even now that we know that the two little squares are identical, we cannot help but see them as being different. The impact of the background and

Through framing, the autopilot and its implicit processes determine how we perceive and act upon the world around us.

how this works remains intangible. The background indirectly, and implicitly, changes our perception and, hence, changes our decisions. This is how the autopilot and pilot work together. They are intertwined. The autopilot provides the frame and the pilot focuses on the figure. Together they create how we experience the world and build the basis for our decision making.

This framing effect is crucial for marketing. With the model we currently use in marketing the impact of the jar on the product experience is hard to explain. The same applies to brands. We know that they have an impact, but how brands work is hard to grasp – they are intangible assets. Framing explains how brands influence purchase decisions: brands operate as the background, framing the perception and, with it, the experience of the products. We know a lot about what people explicitly want from a shampoo, a bank or a car (the small grey square). What is more difficult to grasp is the interplay between the brand working as a background and the product on which the consumer focuses. Framing explains the real equity of brands for selling products. We know this from blind tests: branded products appear superior to unbranded although, objectively, the product is identical. This framing effect of brands is not marketing hype; it increases the perceived value and the willingness to pay a premium price – even for objectively identical products. The VW Sharan and the Ford Galaxy are identical cars – both produced in the same factories – but consumers have been willing to spend a premium of €2,000 for the frame that the VW brand added. In the UK, Virgin Mobile has higher perceived network quality and satisfaction scores than T-Mobile despite the fact that it uses the exact same network.

Starbucks can command a significant price premium for its coffee. Let's think about what frame the brand conveys: the interior design is warm

Figure 1.8 The Starbucks brand frame justifies its price premium

and cosy, the smells are exotic, and world music is playing in the background. There is a Starbucks everywhere in the world. A visit to Starbucks is more than just a momentary 'pit stop' (what Wild Bean Café offers), it is a short getaway to the 'third place' between home and work. The Starbucks brand, one could say, frames the coffee experience as 'a short holiday' (see Figure 1.8).

The 'short holiday' frame is both credible and intuitive as it is 'baked in' to coffee itself: the smells, the exotic varieties, the special modes of preparation – coffee as a product is the right bridge to this frame of reference. The frame can be different depending on the culture. For example, in China Starbucks is not about a short holiday but rather a symbol for status and a visit indicates social wealth. This had a significant impact on the sales pattern because people stayed there in order to be seen and consequently did not buy coffee to take away. Because of this frame and its impact on consumer behaviour, Starbucks increased the shop size in order to accommodate more people and compensate for the low volume in takeaway sales.

It is unlikely that in a blind test consumers would be able to judge a difference in taste or quality of a Starbucks coffee versus its competitors. Nevertheless people are willing to pay a significant price premium for the frame that the brand and the outlet provide. This implicit value that the frame adds is exactly what we've meant all along by the intangible asset we call 'brand equity'. The amount of money that we are prepared to pay over and above the objective value of the product is exactly equal to the value of the frame that the brand provides at the moment of purchase. A quick calculation of the margin this provides per cup of coffee multiplied by the millions of cups that Starbucks sells every year shows that this matters hugely to the commercial success of a business and by far outweighs the marketing support budget.

The Virgin Mobile example indicates that framing works not only for tangible products like coffee or cars but also for intangibles such as network quality. In fact, one can argue that brands as frames for products are especially important for intangible offers like services, data transfer (e.g. high-speed internet) or content because quality and value are hard to judge, and even harder to compare, in these cases. For these industries brand frames are a crucial lever for differentiation. That brands are important for intangibles is also shown by a recent list of the most valuable brands produced by market research agency Millward Brown. The majority of brands in the Top 20 are in the IT, telecommunications and service (e.g. banking) businesses. Here the brand makes the difference, because the product or service offered is intangible and hence hard to evaluate – so the perceived value is strongly determined by the frame.

A brain-imaging study by the University of Munster published in the trade journal *Brain Research Bulletin* (Deppe *et al.* 2005) shows how media

THE ⚜ TIMES

**RAIL TICKET
PRICES
TO DOUBLE
NEXT YEAR**

**RAIL TICKET
PRICES
TO DOUBLE
NEXT YEAR**

Figure 1.9 The media brand frame influences credibility. Images reproduced with permission of NI Syndication

brands influence the credibility of a news item through framing (see Figure 1.9). The researchers evaluated news items in terms of their credibility. During this process they presented the news either with a brand background (brand logos and typefaces from well-known magazines) or without the media brand (as an isolated 'figure').

The result clearly showed that the credibility of an identical news item was strongly influenced by the background frame of reference in which the news was presented. Depending on the media brand in the background, the subjective credibility changed massively – without the respondents being aware of the reason for this. The study showed that the framing effect operates in areas of the brain whose functioning we do not consciously experience. In addition, this effect happens very quickly – the brains of the respondents had made their judgement about the credibility of a news item long before the person had even finished reading it and was able to make a judgement on reflection. All of this was triggered by the brand signals in the background. The autopilot works very fast, so that the logo was processed by the autopilot system in a fraction of a second and this framed the news item. Subjectively, the respondents based their judgement only on the news items because the impact of the auto-pilot system, the framing, remains implicit. The explicit judgement about the credibility of a news item was therefore massively influenced, and coloured, by the implicit processes in the autopilot.

The perspective of 'brands as frames' can help to end the typical dualistic debate between Marketing and Sales departments, where Sales want to focus on the product while Marketing and agencies want to put the focus on a brand's 'image'. This dualism often translates into a discussion (or argument) as to how much product should be shown in an ad (features, facts, text) and how much time and space should be allocated to the brand (images, stories, emotions). When creating communication, we often think of brand and product as antagonists: it is brand *or* product, sales *or* image, functional *or* emotional benefit. This dualism originates in the outdated 'emotional versus rational' model of decision making which we use – mostly without being aware of it – to conceptualize the roles of brand (emotional) and product (rational) in purchase decisions. In the new view, brand and product are not antagonists, they are intertwined: brands provide the background which increases the perceived value of the product. If you remove the grey square at the centre (the product) then you have nothing of value at all. The substance is lacking. Figure 1.10 shows what

Figure 1.10 Without the brand frame, products appear identical

happens if you remove the frame (the brand): there is only the product left and we all know that, particularly in mature markets, the quality at the product level hardly offers a perceivable and big enough difference between competing products, as indicated by the success of private labels. And since, in most categories, customers are quite satisfied with the product performance, a relevant differentiation at the pure product level is increasingly hard to provide.

The idea that there is something more to how brands and products are experienced and perceived than purely their objective qualities is not new in itself. This 'added value' of brands explains the high sums that companies are prepared to pay when acquiring other companies' brands. In the Coca-Cola Company's 2011 annual report they place a 25 per cent higher value on goodwill and trademarks (i.e. intangible assets like their brands) than on their tangible assets (property, plant and equipment). However, until now, it was hard to capture and define precisely what is meant by this branded effect – although there are many descriptions given to it, such as intangible, hidden, unconscious, psychological, emotional or irrational. The core benefit of modern decision science is to provide an analytical, systematic access to the autopilot system and, hence, to the implicit level of purchase decision making and its intertwining with the explicit level.

Brands are frames: they implicitly influence the perceived value of products and product experience through framing.

Why we underestimate the influence of the implicit level

Although we'll quite happily pay three times more for a scoop of ice cream or for a cup of coffee than the cost of the product itself would objectively justify, the brand is only rarely mentioned by consumers as a reason for purchase. We have already seen that we don't have access to how exactly the frame influences our perception of the small grey square. One study by GfK examined the reasons for purchasing watches. Several 'typologies' of watch buyers were identified. The study identified those 'fixated on materials' as the most important type of buyer. They decide on a particular watch because they like the material. Brands are not mentioned. But is this result really plausible? How variable can the materials of a watch be? Metal, with a leather or plastic band. When we buy a watch for €200, do we really check out the cut of the metal with a magnifying glass? Are we even actually capable of evaluating this and is it really determinative in our purchase decision? Is it really true that the brand plays no role here?

One could almost be forgiven for thinking so, because the subject of brands does not even appear in the upper price segment. Let's quote from the same study:

'In the upper price segment, meaning watches with a purchase price of at least 350 Euros, the "functional aesthete" takes up the lion's share: around 40 percent of all watches in this price segment are bought by this customer type. What is especially important: the watch has to fulfil additional functions, for example function as a stop watch and show the date.'

Again, no sign of the brand. Really? For a watch in the upper price segment? For a product that carries so much history and cultural significance, which is recognizable to everyone and which makes a statement about us, can it really be true that the date display or stop-watch capability is the decisive factor for purchase?

Suggestion

Consider the following – for which products would you say that the brand triggered the impetus for purchase? What about your watch? Your kitchen appliances? Your furniture? Toothpaste? Coffee?

The pilot system, which we probe through explicit questions, has only limited access to these implicit drivers of purchase decisions. When asked in surveys, customers provide information in great detail about why they choose this shampoo or that service. They are not wrong, but they tell us only about the explicit part of the decision making. In the jar study the customers talked about the performance of the cream and the price – and this is not wrong – but this introspection is just not the complete picture. The influence of the frame that the autopilot system provides remains implicit. We do not have conscious access to the workings of the autopilot, so these answers most likely are not the full picture.

The framing effect explains why the brand effects are so frequently underestimated in surveys, because framing operates indirectly and we aren't aware of its influence. Hence, when we're asked about our reasons for buying a watch, we think of product characteristics (the small grey square) and not the brand (the background frame). The reason is that the effect of the background is not perceptible. We simply don't notice the subtle, but massive, radiating effect of the background.

What is so fascinating is that the autopilot frames decisions without us noticing. It operates in areas of the brain whose work we're hardly aware of, if at all. But a brand's appeal exists exactly because of this background. In order to understand and control the effect of brands, we therefore have to decode this indirect influence of the autopilot.

The impact of frames, and thus brands, on our behaviour is implicit and we therefore do not consciously experience it.

Science box

The neurological basis of pilot and autopilot

Despite it being problematic to attribute complex functions like those of the pilot or autopilot to anatomical structures, we can roughly locate the most important brain areas for both systems. The pilot's work is based on, among others, the dorso-lateral prefrontal cortex at the very front of the brain, in the frontal lobe. It is assumed that the centre of working memory is contained in this brain area, which we use, for example, when we consider where to spend our next holiday. Also part of the pilot is the anterior cingulate cortex, which among other functions also registers and reacts to conflicts and disturbances of the autopilot.

The autopilot is based on a multitude of neurostructures, which have the common feature of doing their work mainly implicitly. This includes all sensory areas, the orbitofrontal cortex (OFC, the reward centre), the ventromedial prefrontal cortex (integration of emotion and cognition, self-relevance), the amygdala (an emotional centre) and the basal ganglia (recognize and learn patterns and rewards).

For the interested reader, the following paper by Professor Matthew Lieberman of UCLA gives an excellent overview of the neural basis of System 1 and System 2.

Lieberman, M.D. (2007). Social cognitive neuroscience: A review of core processes. *Annual Review of Psychology, 58,* 259–289.

Decoding the autopilot

In the last 20 years, science has gained a huge amount of knowledge about the architecture and functionality of the implicit system. This new under-standing of the implicit level of decision making is based on robust and accurate measurement techniques able to measure implicit processes with sufficient objectivity and precision. Such techniques include priming para-digms from psychology, or imaging techniques from neuroscience such as fMRI (functional magnetic resonance imaging). Thanks to the progress in methodology and theory the implicit level is no longer considered to be the 'harassing fires of immoral impulses' as Freudian theory suggested. Let's have a look at the aspects with which the autopilot deals. We will get back to each of these in later chapters, but it can help if we get a feeling for the scope of the autopilot's processing even at this early stage on our journey.

As the Kahneman model illustrates, the first module in the autopilot is perception through our five senses. Perception is the key interface to our marketing activities, be it the benefits of our products, the brand, the smell of our face cream, the size or colour of our packaging, or the testimonial and music we use in our TV ads. The prerequisite for all of this to have an impact is that it gets inside consumers' minds, and perception is the door through which our products and brands have to enter. In order for our messages to have an impact, they first need to be perceived. Perception largely operates at an implicit level: we have no clue exactly how we are able to recognize a red traffic light within a fraction of a second, or which processes in our brain are responsible for this. We just see the red light as if we had a camera sitting on our eyes. However, as we will see in Chapter 3, the reality could not be further from this notion of 'perception as a camera'. Perception is an active process in the autopilot, as the framing effect shows: the colour of the little squares is objectively identical but our brain makes them appear different.

How we actively create, rather than passively perceive, the world around us is illustrated by the following experiment. Consumers were given a vanilla pudding that had been made to look brown by using tasteless food colouring, so that it closely resembled a chocolate pudding visually. The consumers were asked to taste it and, in doing so, to describe how it tasted. The fascinating outcome was that what they reported had nothing to do with what they, objectively, were eating – most of them described the taste of chocolate. They all subjectively experienced what they implicitly expected, misled by the appearance of the pudding.

Subjects in a related study who believed they had been given standard coffee showed an increased pulse and heart rate even if they had, in fact, been given decaffeinated coffee. This explains the difference in performance experienced by consumers when using their preferred brand as opposed to an unbranded equivalent, even though the two basic products might be exactly the same – the brand frame activates expectations, and these, in turn, influence the subjective, perceived product experience without us being aware of this influence. Our perception, and hence our product experience, is created mainly by implicit processes in the autopilot.

The pudding experiment shows that expectations are part of the autopilot. We expect a brown pudding to taste like chocolate and this expectation modulates, in the background, the subjective taste experience. In addition to implicit expectations, there are implicit attitudes. Attitudes about products and brands play an important role in marketing. We measure attitudes such as sympathy, trust or quality because, if consumers have a positive attitude towards our brands, then they are more likely to be considered. However, there are two levels of attitude: explicit and implicit. In a study we measured the explicit and implicit attitudes of two competitors in the banking industry, as shown in Figure 1.11.

If we look at the explicit image, the profiles of both brands are correlated twice as much (r = .64) compared with the implicit profiles (r = .30). This comes as no surprise because we have already seen that the true differences between the brands come to the fore only when the frame is present. Only

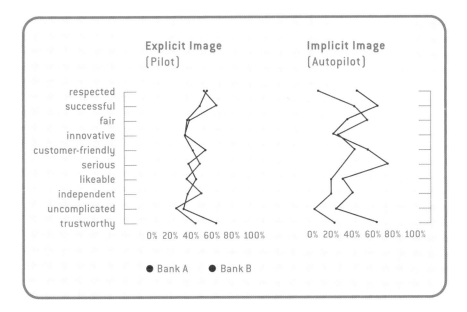

Figure 1.11 The explicit and implicit image profiles are very different

when adding the frame – the implicit level – do we get the complete picture and a much stronger differentiation between the brands emerges.

Another example is shown through consumers' attitudes regarding healthy food. While most of us have positive attitudes towards healthy food at an explicit level, the autopilot has a different take. In a study published in the *Journal of Marketing* in 2006, it was found that the less a product was presented as, or perceived to be, healthy, the better its taste ratings were before, during and after consumption. The autopilot uses the rule 'unhealthy = tasty'. This implicit attitude frames the experience irrespective of the stated, explicit attitude. It works for people who will tell you that unhealthy food is tasty, and with people who don't believe this rule explicitly. It explains the failure of Pizza Hut's low-cal pizza or the fat-reduced McLean burgers – the subjective taste changes when we eat a burger that we know contains less fat.

In a similar way, consumers in the UK had expectations, created by years of instant coffee advertising, that granules, as a product format, were superior in taste and quality to the same product in powdered form. This expectation then transferred across categories such that, when Unilever researched instant soups, consumers rated those soups which they were told were made from granules as significantly better than other soups which they were informed had been made from powder – even though the two soups were identical.

The autopilot also contains a large number of our motivational drivers. Beside our explicit motivations, there is also an implicit motivational level. We may, for example, have the goal of buying detergent to clean our laundry. Beside this explicit goal, there is also an implicit level of motivation connected with the purchase decision, as the following study shows.

The autopilot manages the majority of perceptions, expectations, attitudes and motivational drivers underlying purchase decisions

In an experiment, some of the respondents were involved in a situation where they had to tell a lie. After the experiment they were free to choose from several products such as soft drinks, cookies or disinfectant wipes. Those respondents who told lies chose the disinfectant wipes significantly more often than those who didn't. In a subsequent, linked study the scientist measured the time the respondents took to wash their hands as the main variable. It turned out that respondents who were asked to lie washed their hands for a significantly longer time compared with respondents in the neutral condition. This experiment shows that cleaning is implicitly linked with guilt and morality. As we will see later in the book, such implicit motivational drivers in the autopilot strongly influence purchase decisions – and this offers a huge opportunity for brand management.

So we have reached the first stop in our journey to understanding the why of consumer behaviour. What has emerged is that we have an analytical framework to manage the explicit and implicit level of decision making. Let's now see how we can build on this to increase the efficacy of marketing.

What we have learned in this chapter

- We can distinguish between two decision-making systems at work in any decision we make: an implicit system working like an auto-pilot, and an explicit system operating like a pilot.
- Together these two systems determine our perception of products and brands and our purchase decisions.
- The implicit autopilot system influences our decisions through an indirect, yet powerful, framing effect.

What this means to us as marketers

- To fully understand consumer decision making, and to persuade consumers to buy our products or services, we need to take into account both the explicit and the implicit levels of decisions.
- While we always knew that there were more than just explicit drivers behind our decisions, it was always hard to identify and manage this more implicit level. We now have a systematic and analytical approach to manage the implicit level of purchase decisions.
- The enormous capacity of the autopilot provides us with a new and exciting opportunity to influence behaviour. Potentially all the signals that we send can increase the persuasiveness of our marketing activities.

2

The Moment of Truth

Decoding Purchase Decisions

We have seen that there are two systems driving our decisions, the autopilot and the pilot. But when we are standing in front of a shelf in a supermarket or comparing alternative service providers, how do we arrive at our decision? What determines whether we buy one brand or another? How do we choose between all the different options? In this chapter we deep-dive into these crucial questions and unlock the underlying principles of purchase decisions.

The neuro-logic of a purchase decision

The role of marketers is to influence consumer behaviour, both short- and long-term, in favour of the brands they manage. We need to retain our customer base, increase purchase frequency and turn non-users into users. Therefore the question of why consumers buy what they buy, and the search for what it is that determines their choices, are at the core of marketing.

In a ground-breaking experiment (see Figure 2.1), neuroscientist Brian Knutson, Professor at Stanford University, and his colleagues (2007) wanted to find out if it was possible to predict purchase behaviour by analyzing neural activity. His research began with images of products and brands – for example a box of chocolates –shown for a few seconds. Then, additionally, the price appeared on the screen, and finally the respondents had to state, by pushing a button, whether they would buy the chocolates or not.

Brain activities were measured the entire time using brain imaging (fMRI). This showed that the picture of the product or brand increases the activation of the so-called 'reward system', which is known to be triggered when we value something. It's as if the brain says, 'I want to have this.' This wanting is based upon the value that we expect the product to deliver. In our associative memory we have experiences with the brand – from using

Brand/Product	Price	Decision
Godiva Chocolate	Godiva Chocolate Price $?	Godiva Chocolate Price $? Yes No
4 sec.	4 sec.	4 sec.

Figure 2.1 Illustration of the classic neuro-economics study 'Neural predictors of purchases' by Knutson and his colleagues from Stanford University

it directly or indirectly, from processing its advertising or from seeing other people using it. Based on this associative learning we have an expected value delivered by the brand. If this expected value is high, then the reward system shows a high level of activation. If the value is low, then the level of activation will also be low.

Now what happened when the price was also shown? When the price was exposed to the respondents, an entirely different area of the brain was activated, namely the insula. This area is normally activated when we experience pain – for example, when we cut our finger (physical pain) or if we are excluded from a group (social pain). In other words, when looking at price, the brain experiences pain – so that means that price isn't anything rational. Price is hot! Price is pain. To explain this we have to be aware that there is no 'shopping' module in the brain, nor is there a 'buy button' or a brand module. Rather, the brain has to 'decide' which of its existing neural modules, all developed for reasons totally different than shopping, should deal with products, brands and prices. The result makes intuitive sense. Products and brands reward us because they help us to achieve our goals. Prices imply giving away something we already own, and which is of significant value to us: money. That this is coded as a painful experience seems reasonable.

The scientists then uncovered the underlying principle that determines whether the brand or product will be bought or not. The principle they found is strikingly straightforward: if the relation between reward and pain exceeds a certain value, the respondents are willing to purchase this item for this price. Our brain calculates a kind of 'net value' and if this is high enough, if the difference between reward and pain is great enough, then we buy. Based on this principle the scientists were able to accurately predict whether the respondents would buy these products or not, hence the title of their paper, 'Neural predictors of purchases'.

Knutson's results show that purchase decisions are based on a reward–pain relationship. This means that in marketing we have two levers to influence consumer decision making – reward and pain – and that they can be independently addressed. In order to make consumers buy, we can increase reward and at the same time decrease pain. It's not uncommon, though, for marketers to adopt a dualistic mindset. For us, the question is whether to focus on the brand or, for example, on a special price offer, as if there were a dilemma in doing both. There isn't. The goal is to increase the 'net value' the brain calculates based on the expected reward of the product and the price. This enables the same piece of advertising to focus on the value that the brand or service offers but also to include a 'hard sell' price message (such as 'for a limited period 30% off'). The first message increases the expected reward, the second reduces the pain, and the unity of both increases the net value.

This simple but fundamental basis of decision making explains why Starbucks can command a premium price for its coffee, or why some people will pay three-figure sums for designer sunglasses. The reward triggered by the brand increases the perceived value, which makes us less resistant to the higher price. The price is higher but, correspondingly, the reward is too, so that, subjectively, a better value–cost relationship exists than that for cheap sunglasses.

The neuro-logic of a purchase decision is based on the equation: net value = reward – pain. The higher the net value, the more likely the purchase.

How to increase value

We know a lot about the explicit value that a product needs to deliver. For example, a shower gel needs to clean, it must smell good, it has to produce foam and so on. Consumers have no problem telling us what they want at a functional level. The challenge is that all shower gels in the market deliver this basic value, and differentiation at this level is hard to achieve – and 'cleans better' is even harder to communicate. Now let's look at the 'Dynamic Pulse' shower gel from Adidas (see Figure 2.2).

Figure 2.2 The packaging of 'Dynamic Pulse' shower gel from Adidas increases net value by influencing the expected reward

It is still a shower gel, fulfilling all the explicit needs that consumers have. But in this case the packaging adds extra value through framing. The context in which the product delivers its value is that of taking a shower. This ritual can entail many different rewards: re-energizing, calming, new start, renewal, etc. Against this background, how does the packaging add value? When we look at the shape it is reminiscent of motor oil. The grip indicates good control and implies a powerful grasp. In addition, a noticeable click can be heard when the product is opened. This packaging design communicates an additional, more implicit, value through the shape, the bottle, the opening sound and the name 'Dynamic Pulse'. It increases the instrumentality of a shower with this product – to refuel and kick-start. It makes the shower a more energizing experience because all of these signals are processed by the 11 million bits of the autopilot and they increase the overall net value of the product in the consumer's mind.

So, in this example, the explicit and implicit values connect perfectly, at least for consumers who want their shower to have an energizing effect. For customers who want a relaxing shower the perceived value will be low because this particular framing does not fit with their motivation.

The explicit value is clear and well understood because we can ask consumers about it. The implicit value, however, often goes unnoticed, and hence unmentioned, by the consumer. As such there is a danger that it is underestimated. But this implicit value offers a huge potential for relevant differentiation and is much harder for competitors to copy. What is it that makes an Apple design prototypically Apple? This is much harder to decode and, hence, difficult to copy.

Let's assume that we're looking for a way to increase value in a commodity category such as drinking water. Our first reflex may well be to think of new additives, such as flavouring the water. Certainly a good approach, but very easy for other brands and private labels to copy, so the competitive edge from a new flavour would not really be sustainable. Voss, the

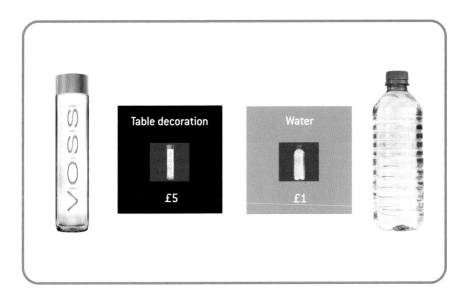

Figure 2.3 The Voss frame achieves high net value despite the high price. Voss image supplied with permission of Voss of Norway ASA. Bottle of water © Thumb/istockphoto.com

branded water from Norway (see Figure 2.3), took a different approach. It increased perceived value significantly, despite the fact that in blind tests even wine experts could not tell the difference between Voss and tap water. But thanks to design language Voss is more than simply water: the implicit value offered by the brand is that of a premium table decoration. This additional value is partly based on the fact that a nicely decorated table uplifts the whole dining experience for those having a meal. This is why it is sold in bars and restaurants. In addition, our autopilot has learned that stars like Madonna drink it because it is so pure, it comes from Norway and it is available only in the most chic and fashionable places.

The associations we build with the product are therefore not only based on our own experiences but the autopilot processes who drinks it and where it is available as well. The autopilot also processes social context. Research in social psychology clearly shows the power of social context

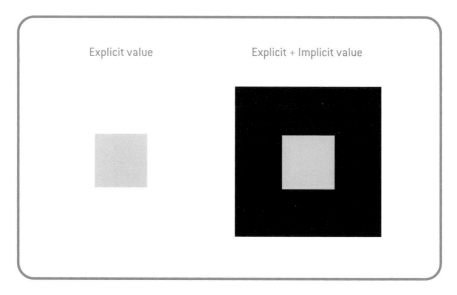

Figure 2.4 Total value increases through implicit frames

to influence purchase behaviour. Seeing or reading about what others do, who is using the product and where it is being used changes the perceived value of Voss above and beyond the effect of the bottle design itself.

So, in order to fully understand purchase decisions we need to consider the value–cost relationship on both levels – the explicit and the implicit (see Figure 2.4).

The classic economics perspective on value and costs is in line with the explicit decision-making process (pilot system): consumers reflectively evaluate the information, judge the quality of the argument, focus on the real, objective facts, and base their decision on reasoning, intentions and attitudes. The autopilot's implicit decision-making process is also based on value and costs. But this system is sensitive to peripheral signals, to expectations, habits and heuristics, to internal states and to the context in which the decision is made.

To maximize net value we need to maximize both the explicit and the implicit value.

Price can increase perceived value

The huge price premium of Voss exploits another implicit rule that we have all learned: the higher the quality, the higher the price. Prices can, and do, signal value. When talking about prices and how they are processed and perceived, we naturally focus on the cost side of the value–cost equation. Indeed, we saw earlier that prices trigger the pain area in the brain. However, prices also influence the value side of the equation as well. For consumers the price is also a guiding signal to evaluate product quality because they have learned – whether it is objectively true or not – that 'quality has its price'.

The impact of price as a quality signal is more powerful than merely to raise or lower explicit expectations. German neuro-economist Hilke Plassmann ran an experiment that looked at the impact of price on the 'real' product experience, i.e. on the physiological response in the brain when consuming differently priced products. Participants were drinking wine while lying in a brain scanner (yes, it's possible!). They were told the price of each wine they tried. What they did not know was that sometimes during the test, they were given the identical wine twice, once with a high price tag ($80), once with a low price tag ($10). Plassmann's research showed that participants rated the higher-priced wine as tasting significantly better, and that this coincided with a marked increase of activity in the brain's reward centre.

Participants did not consciously realize the influence that the price had. This means that price is not only an explicit signal for quality, and therefore pays into the value side of the equation, but this same signal can increase the subjective quality of the product experience. However, there is a precondition for this effect. The price contributes to the perceived value only when the price range within the category is high. Wine can vary in price between about £4 and hundreds of pounds. For shampoos, however, the price range is narrow so that the potential to add perceived value through price alone is rather limited. In the case of Voss, they really increased the price per bottle to the degree where the autopilot cannot help but think, 'It needs to be superb water if it is so much more expensive.' The design, the exclusivity and the stories about Madonna provide a credible foundation for this. Just increasing prices to the maximum would not work by itself.

Language can increase perceived value

So brands, design, packaging and even social information can add complementary implicit value. This is also true for language. Language is an important vehicle in our everyday marketing work that we use to convey our messages. We think a lot about product names, we describe the product in written concepts and we try to persuade the consumer via text on packs or headlines in adverts. So what can we learn from science regarding the impact of language on perceived value?

In a study by Brian Wansink of Cornell University, menus were presented either with descriptive labels such as 'Traditional Cajun Red Beans with Rice', 'Succulent Italian Seafood Filet' and 'Tender Grilled Chicken', or with labels with just the name on it (e.g. 'red beans with rice'). The question was whether such flowery modifiers would have any impact on the perceived taste (i.e. value) of the food. The result was that the descriptive labels not only resulted in more orders but also led participants to rate those foods as tasting better than the identical foods given only a generic name. Of course, we do not explicitly think 'I prefer food served with vivid adjectives', yet a dish's description turns out to be an important factor in how it tastes. What the flowery titles did was to activate value expectations. When we look at the packs in the supermarket, many of them contain text that purely describes what it is (e.g. 'vegetable soup') instead of activating expectations of what we experience when we purchase and consume the product. A 'tender grilled chicken' is perceived to provide higher value than just a 'grilled chicken'.

Value-oriented language can not only add perceived value, it can influence the perceived product performance as well. In a test of messaging on meat packaging, the signal '75 per cent lean' was valued significantly more positively than the message '25 per cent fat'. Interestingly, this higher value persisted when the meat was consumed, meaning that the description influences not only the purchase decision but also the subjective experience of the product.

This impact of language can also be seen on a neuronal level, in particular in the brain region responsible for the valuation of reward: the orbitofrontal cortex (sitting directly behind our eyes). In one study the medial orbitofrontal cortex was more strongly activated when a flavour stimulus was labelled 'rich and delicious flavour' than when it was labelled 'boiled vegetable water'. In another experiment, a standard test odour, isovaleric acid, with a small amount of cheese flavour, was delivered while participants were lying in a brain scanner. On some trials the test odour was accompanied by the label 'cheddar cheese', which was visually presented, and on other trials by the label 'body odour'. It was found that the activation in the OFC in response to the standard test odour was much greater when the label was cheddar cheese than when it was body odour. Moreover, the labels influenced the subjective ratings of how pleasant the test odour was, and the variations in ratings were correlated with the activations in the OFC. Neuroscientist Edmund T. Rolls (2006) summarizes these findings as follows:

Part of the interest and importance of this finding is that it shows that cognitive influences, originating here purely at the word-level, can reach down and modulate activations in the first stage of cortical processing that represents the value of sensory stimuli.

A helpful distinction to describe product benefits or promotions is the one between gain and non-loss. These are two sides of the same coin: 'gain' addresses what people receive, 'non-loss' addresses the benefits of not losing or not missing out on something. In the cosmetics category, where the goal is to change and achieve something, a gain focus makes sense, such as 'get that summer beach look with Bronze Goddess from Estée Lauder'. Non-loss is important in risky environments. Anxiety caused by the recent financial crises and the risk of inflation eroding savings, for example, is used by estate agents to urge people to invest in property in order not to lose their money. A gain-oriented 'return on investment' would not be as effective in times of economic recession. Consider the examples in Figure 2.5 of typical words that can be used for gain and non-loss, for example in promotions.

Non-loss	Gain
No risk /Free	Plus
Do not pay too much	Get
No more than	Discover
Only	Win
Money back if unsatisfied	Extra
Avoid	More
Without	Play
Reduced ...	Help ...

Figure 2.5 Two basic ways to increase perceived value: gain frame and non-loss frame

Suggestion

Which of the two frames do you tend to use in your marketing communication?

Reducing perceived cost

The same principles and mechanisms which increase perceived value can be used for managing price perception: as with value, there is an explicit and an implicit level of cost. The explicit level of cost is clear: it is the objective price point. But even here there is an implicit level. Instead of changing (e.g. lowering) the real price, we can change the perceived price with appropriate contextual signals which the autopilot 'understands'.

Take a look at Figure 2.6. As the figure shows, the price with a shiny star is rated as the most expensive, much more so than if this same price was presented as black on white. In turn, black on white is rated as more expensive than a price with a discount symbol next to it, or if the 'old' price is shown as crossed out. Objectively, the price is always the same, but the valuation of the 'pain' is different due to its presentation and, therefore, the impact is very different. Research shows that a price given a promotional 'flash', even if that price has been increased, will result in higher sales because the flash lowers the perceived cost. As we will see in

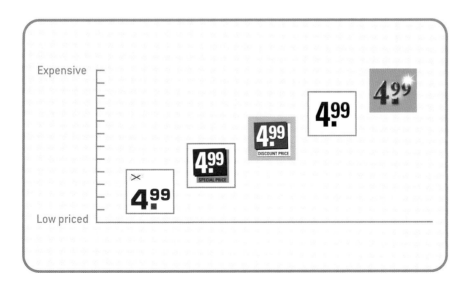

Figure 2.6 The way price is presented makes a difference

the next chapter, price perception is inherently relativistic and therefore can be affected by the context in which the price is perceived. So the judgement of the price is heavily influenced by implicit signals.

Another approach to reduce perceived cost is a mechanism called 'anchoring'. When Steve Jobs introduced the iPad, he showed off its features and then asked: 'What should we price it at? If you listen to the pundits, we're going to price it at under $1,000.' A giant '$999' came up on his presentation screen. He left it there to sink in before saying, 'I am thrilled to announce to you that the iPad pricing starts not at $999 but at just $499.' Onscreen, the '$999' price was then visibly crushed by a falling '$499'. So the final price point appeared to be a very good deal – it reduced the perceived cost. What Jobs deliberately did not do was to compare the iPad price with that of a notebook – he compared it with the expectation of its own price. In so doing he removed notebooks as a reference point for both pricing and performance/features, thereby maintaining the uniqueness of his product. The first price is the anchor and the next price is evaluated relative to this anchor.

This anchoring mechanism, by which price perception can be influenced by contrasting it against other prices, is very robust. Take negotiations, for example. Buyer–seller negotiation experiments have repeatedly demonstrated that final outcomes are consistently and positively anchored by the first offer. Many studies show that when selling products, it often makes sense to follow a 'starting high and ending low' strategy: show people the highest-priced option first to set an anchor for subsequent, cheaper options.

In his excellent book on price perception, *Priceless: The Myth of Fair Value*, William Poundstone describes a fascinating field experiment run by MIT scientists with a mail-order company. Using 'charm prices' that end in a '9' is very common, and this company is no exception. They sell women's clothing and normally used whole-dollar prices ending in a 9. One of the items tested was priced at $39. Different, experimental, versions of the mail-order catalogue were produced, and the company offered the same item for $34 and $44. Each catalogue was sent to a random, and identically sized, sample sourced from the company's existing mailing list. There were more sales at the $39 price than either of the other two prices – 23 per cent more people bought the dress priced at $39 than at $34. Interestingly, there was no significant difference in sales when a garment was priced at $44 or $34.

The catalogue company frequently put items on sale and marked them, in their catalogues, with the old and new prices: 'Regular price $X SALE $Y.' As part of the experiment, they also printed some catalogues containing the sale prices but without any indication that they were actually discounted. As one might expect, they saw higher unit sales when the sale prices were highlighted as such. Consumers didn't know that $Y was a bargain price unless the catalogue told them it was by anchoring it against the higher, non-sale, price. But they also found that sales price markers were more powerful than the 'charm' prices. Consumers were more likely to buy an item for $40 if an anchor of the regular price of $48 was salient than if the same item cost $39 with no other anchor.

As with value, there are two levels of price perception: explicit and implicit. The explicit price is the objective price point. The implicit price is determined by how the price is presented.

Money is not the only cost

Besides money there is another type of cost: time. If you're in a service business then loss of time can significantly increase the perceived cost side of the value–cost relation for your customers. What we've seen so far that applies to prices and numbers is also true for time: perceived time is relative. When we travel by train to meet a good friend, time seems to fly, whereas we experience it as dragging by when we have screaming kids around us after a long working day. Decreasing actual waiting time can be very costly for a business (for example, having more service personnel available), so the opportunity to influence the perception of waiting time is a valuable alternative.

There are validated triggers with which perceived waiting time can be decreased. First, once we have started a service process, i.e. we've logged our problem, then we're prepared to wait longer because the process has already started. As such, getting a customer to this stage as quickly as possible is important. Second, no one wants to lose or waste time so, in order to prevent this perception, if we can give customers something to do that is of value to them they will view it as 'time well spent' rather than time lost. Some garages offer clean and pleasant waiting areas where customers can watch TV, read newspapers, use WiFi and help themselves to free drinks. A third hint is to give reasons for the wait – thus serving the pilot – leading to better evaluation of service quality even though the objective waiting time may still be the same. In general, an important driver is to reduce – or better still remove – uncertainty: we are much happier to wait for 9 minutes for a train if we know that it will arrive in 9 minutes, than to wait for 5 minutes not knowing when the next train will arrive.

Finally, there is yet another perspective on price and cost: behavioural costs. Perceived cost is also based on the amount of effort necessary to buy or consume a product. One famous example is the '300 Million Dollar' button, mentioned by Luke Wroblewski in his book *Web Form Design: Filling in the Blank*. By making a simple change in the path to purchase, a website increased its sales by 45 per cent, producing an additional $15 million revenue in the first month alone. For the first year, the site saw an additional $300 million in sales. So what happened? Before the change, users had to register with their email address before they could check out. Returning visitors could use this to log in. The team designed it this way as their intention was to enable repeat customers to purchase faster. Their view was that first-time purchasers wouldn't mind the extra effort of registering because subsequent purchases would be much faster and easier. However, first-time buyers actually hated having to register before purchasing. Some, who couldn't remember whether it was their first purchase, became frustrated as their usual email and password combination failed. Even repeat customers weren't any happier as most couldn't remember their login details. In fact, as many as 45 per cent of all customers had multiple registrations in the system, with some having registered ten times. Of the 160,000 passwords requested every day, 75 per cent never went on to complete the purchase. The web registration form, which was intended to make shopping easier, actually prevented countless sales.

The solution was simple. The designers removed the 'Register' button. In its place, they put a 'Continue' button with the simple message: 'You do not need to create an account to make purchases on our site. Simply click Continue to proceed to checkout. To make your future purchases even faster, you can create an account during checkout.'

Focusing on the ease of doing business with a company can be very effective, as the car insurance brand Geico has found. In their advertising campaign, which has been running since 2004, they make a virtue of the low level of behavioural cost involved in using their website. They show a Neanderthal caveman in a modern setting, with the strapline 'So easy, a caveman could do it'.

There are two types of costs: monetary and behavioural. Behavioural costs include the amount of time and effort required to obtain a reward.

As these examples illustrate, identifying and reducing behavioural costs is a big lever for optimizing the path to purchase. It also shows that many barriers in this path originate in the interface with which we provide people, in these cases the website and the sequence of steps in the shopping process.

Value–cost relation is relative

Look at Figure 2.7. Is the circle big or small?

The answer is: it depends. This example illustrates a basic principle of how we value products and brands. We judge the value of a choice relative

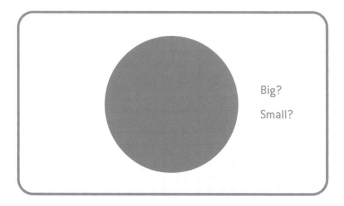

Figure 2.7 We cannot judge the size of the circle without a reference

to the other options available. When we are hot and thirsty and the only thing available is a warm Coke, we will value this option very highly. If we have the choice between the warm Coke and a cold beer, the value of the warm Coke is significantly reduced. Some time ago *The Economist* communicated the following offer on its website (this example comes from Dan Ariely's bestselling book *Predictably Irrational* [2010]). Each price was for a one-year subscription:

Web-only: US $59.00
Print-only: US $125.00
Print & web: US $125.00

We may not know whether the web-only subscription at $59 is a better deal than the print-only subscription at $125; however, we certainly understand that the print & web option for $125 is a better deal than the print-only option for the same price. Indeed, only 16 per cent of subscribers chose the web-only option; the majority of 84 per cent opted for the print & web subscription. Not surprisingly, no one picked the print-only subscription. If there's an option that no one wants, we might be forgiven for thinking that we should delete this option from our offering. So this is what they then tried:

Web-only: US $59.00
Print & web: US $125.00

What happened to subscriptions under these conditions? The least popular version become the most popular, and vice versa: the web-only option, originally chosen by only 16 per cent, was now chosen by 68 per cent, while the print & web option, which 84 per cent picked in the original version, was now chosen by only 32 per cent.

For *The Economist* this is a lower-value mix of subscription revenue compared with the offer with three options. Having three options rather than two means that the total value of subscriptions from 100 subscribers rises from $8,012 to $11,444 – an increase of 43 per cent. What's going on here? The print-only option, which was useless in the sense that no one wanted it, was actually very useful because it influenced the calculation of the value–cost relationship: relative to the option in the middle (only print), the print & web option looked like a great deal.

This example shows a basic but important principle in our brain: the calculation of value is based on contrasting options that are presented in a particular situational context. Simply by changing the structure of the offer, the decisions for the web-only option changed dramatically. This works because value is fundamentally relative. Estate agents work this way. They will show you a house very similar to the one they think you will buy but slightly more expensive and a little worse. It will then be much easier to sell you the house they think you will buy. Many experiments display what has been termed 'coherent arbitrariness', which describes the apparent consistency of behaviour that occurs once otherwise arbitrary baseline values have been set.

One implication of the relativistic nature of value is that we need to pay close attention to direct competitor offers because consumers will base their purchase decision on the relative value we deliver compared with

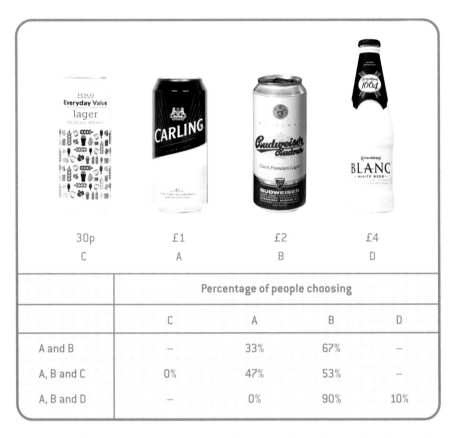

Figure 2.8 The competitive environment determines the relative value of a product

the competition. The table in Figure 2.8 is based on a study by the agency Mountainview. It shows the impact on sales of Carling and Budweiser at £1 and £2, respectively, depending on three scenarios.

1. Scenario offering A and B: 67 per cent buy the Budweiser for £2 while 33 per cent buy the Carling.
2. Scenario offering A, B and C: adds Tesco value lager priced at 30p. Nobody buys it but it pulls the rest of the category down market: now 47 per cent buy the Carling, 53 per cent buy Bud.

3. Scenario offering A, B and D: adds a premium French beer, Kronenbourg, for £4 a bottle, so 10 per cent of people buy that, 90 per cent of people buy the Bud and now nobody buys the Carling.

This shows the extent to which we choose things based on relative rather than absolute value. We choose according to the frame of reference at which we are looking at a given moment in time. Interestingly, if you now think of a goldfish: is it big or small? Small. Why can we judge that more easily compared with the circle? The judgement can be made relative to a learned reference point. We compare the goldfish with the prototypical fish and, based on our experience – more precisely our memory – the goldfish is small compared with a prototypical fish we tend to recall. So even if there is no direct context available, we produce a frame of reference from experience and memory because, otherwise, we cannot judge the value. For example, if we learned that our favourite wine from Spain typically retails at £50 a bottle, we would jump at the chance to buy a bottle for £30, simply because in relative terms it must be a good price. However, when it comes to prices, consumers often do not have clear expectations and knowledge, which means that a concrete frame of reference can have an even higher impact.

Let's look at another example to further elaborate on this important learning. Nespresso manages to achieve a tremendous price premium for its product which cannot be explained by the taste alone. The advertising, the different product experience due to its product form, how it produces coffee using its complementary machines and its exclusivity all form part of the brand's differentiation. However, a key aspect of this successful case that is usually overlooked is the point that Nespresso managed to prevent normal coffee being the consumer's reference frame regarding price. Studies show that if we do not have a direct comparison, we are more likely to accept far higher prices for a product simply because the reference frame is missing. Therefore, selling the coffee capsules via their Nespresso Club not only adds to the exclusive nature of the brand, it has the benefit of not having a concrete reference.

What would have happened if the capsules had been placed directly on a retail shelf next to other coffee packs? Although it is espresso rather than regular coffee, the standard coffee price would have been used as the reference point. Therefore its perceived price would have been much higher than it is without this frame. So what happens instead is that the autopilot – because it depends on contrasting options – searches for another reference frame, and the closest to the product experience is an espresso that we already know from cups of coffee we purchase away from the home (e.g. in a cafeteria or from Starbucks). Compared with this price the 25p for one Nespresso appears relatively cheap. The huge success of the cups and capsules in the market place will establish a new reference frame over time. So it does not come as a surprise that according to Ric Rhinehart, Executive Director of the Specialty Coffee Association of America, the reference point for coffee is increasingly cups, not jars. Americans under the age of 40 are thinking about coffee pricing in cups, while previous generations were thinking about the price per jar.

The reason for the relativity of perceived value originates in the basic principles of perception. If we look at single neurons in the sensory brain, they all have one thing in common: they respond only to differences and changes. If there is no difference or contrast, the receptors stay inactive. The following quote from Nick Chater, Professor of Behavioural Science at Warwick Business School, illustrates the point:

> We have no absolute idea how much we value any object, service or experience, even with excellent information. All we have is comparison between similar things. I compare my present meal with other, similar meals – not with cars, or car journeys, let alone laundry.

This has big implications for how we measure purchase intention as well. Purchase intent is one of the most often used performance indicators in marketing. We often ask consumers for their purchase intent based on this product, that particular concept, advert or pack design without comparing it with those of competitors or even providing the price as a context. Professor Vicki Morwitz and her colleagues from New York University found that measured purchase intention in surveys can be made a much better predictor of sales if the product is placed within its competitive environment and hence the relative value of the offer is exposed. Additionally, providing pricing information for the test product and its competitors improves the results. The reason is that, without this context, we cannot judge the value and the cost intuitively. We start thinking and building our own, potentially biased, reference frame. If people are to evaluate a new product, it is like being asked to judge the size of a goldfish without knowing any other fish. Creative designs or adverts often fail in pre-tests because, without a frame of reference, people tend to have a preference for the familiar and the typical.

We need comparisons to make decisions. Value and cost are fundamentally relativistic.

Occasion-based marketing

Since value and cost are relativistic, they can be significantly influenced by the situational context we are in. When we are thirsty, the relative value of a Coke will be much higher than when we are not thirsty. In general, the value we apply to products and brands is determined by, and relative to, the situation we are in. In psychology, behaviour is summarized as the interaction between situational factors and personal factors. On the one hand, we as individuals have traits, needs and personalities that shape what we value and what we do. On the other hand, we all know that situations can influence behaviour as well – as a basic example, we have different needs on a hot day versus a cold day. In marketing our focus is often on stable personal factors such as preferences, needs and attitudes, independent of the situation. The reasons for this tendency are twofold. One is that, as marketers, we have not had a systematic approach to understand how the outside world, including the situational context, influences

perceived value. The other is that, as humans, we don't consciously perceive how the situation, the environment, influences our behaviour. It is
therefore easy to underestimate the power of context to influence decisions
because, as with framing, we do not notice its influence – it remains
implicit. Thinking about consumer behaviour from a situational rather
than from a personal perspective offers huge potential to understand it.
This offers an additional thread for brand positioning and is an interesting
springboard for innovations. So it does not come as a surprise that leading
companies such as Kraft Foods or Nestlé are adopting occasion-based
marketing. Let's have a look at how the occasion-based perspective
can help.

In a study we did for one of our clients we were analyzing the ice-cream
market. The brand was number two in the market and the client had
been using the standard marketing approaches: the brand was positioned
on specific characteristics and attributes and consumer behaviour was
explained by constructs such as top of mind, consideration set, preferred
brand, loyalty and a trait-based segmentation. Overall their focus was the
consumer, not the situations they were in.

Now, what changes when we take a perspective that focuses on situational
factors? Let's have a look at the top-of-mind construct. Top of mind is
normally measured by asking, 'If you think of an ice-cream brand, which
brand comes to your mind first, second, etc.?' To answer this question,
consumers need to use their memory. Without providing a specific situational context, people use the prototype of ice cream that they've learned
to address this question. But we have already seen that the autopilot
also processes the environment in which we consume products, so our
associative memory integrates situations and occasions into the associative
memory network. Former drug addicts, for example, can experience craving
simply by driving past the place where they used to buy their drugs – the
situational trigger activates craving based solely on memory. Alcoholics
often hide alcohol when they are drunk but cannot remember where they

hid it the next day. However, if they get drunk again, they suddenly recall where it is. Experiments show that if we learn vocabulary under water, our recall is best if we are under water again.

The context plays an important part not only in perception but also in memorizing what we perceive. In our study it turned out that we got different research results if we asked, 'Which ice-cream brand comes to mind if you think of having ice cream as a dessert at Christmas?' compared with if we asked generically which ice-cream brands someone was aware of. Providing a situational frame affects significantly which ice-cream brand is top of mind.

The same principle applies to the consideration set, preferred brand and loyalty. We have already seen that cortical relief occurs only for the most preferred brand, not for the second or third choice. It is not enough merely to be in the relevant consideration set, it is important for a brand to be number one – more precisely to be number one with regards to a specific occasion. In the ice-cream example, the market leader had top-of-mind awareness overall, and was number one in the consideration set. However, the number two brand in the market owned some very important occasions, such as ice cream 'for dessert' and ice cream 'to spoil myself'. Since the revenue potential of the various occasions can be measured, positioning the brand using occasions can be a helpful management tool, helping to identify gaps with high sales potential that are not yet owned by another brand but which offer significant growth potential.

This sheds a different light on loyalty as well. Consumers might show loyalty in respect to certain occasions but low loyalty overall. Therefore an efficient guideline for managing our brands is to know which occasions we want to own – 'own' means that the occasion will evoke our brand first. For the number two or three brand in a market this approach can be more encouraging and fruitful than trying to be number one overall by trying to beat the current market leader at a generic occasion level.

Focusing on an occasion-based approach can also increase a brand's penetration. The usual approach to segmentation is to build segments based on stable preferences, needs, demographics or life cycle. These factors can of course explain behaviour in some categories. However, in those categories where the product is used on different occasions (as is the case with ice cream), or is not bought or used as an extension of the self to signal personality (such as FMCG markets), a segmentation based only on the consumer and not on occasion can limit our understanding and explanation of purchase decisions. When we are 'on the go' with children, we have different needs regarding ice cream than we have when we are on our own, or as a couple in a restaurant. This is true no matter if we are young or old. Crucially, in these cases, it is too restrictive to assign one consumer exclusively to just one segment. They can belong to more than one depending on the occasions.

The occasion-based approach can also help when we are considering launching into new markets. A pharmaceutical company wanted to grow their business by selling a new kind of hay-fever allergy therapy. With such therapy the patients get injections over quite a long period of time in order to desensitize the immune system to the allergens. However, every doctor offering this type of therapy already has a preferred company with which he works. Doctors were already familiar with the current therapy schemata and there is no difference in either efficacy or price between available products. So the perceived value of switching is rather low and the perceived costs are high due to the change of therapy. So the company focused on a specific characteristic of their product: their therapy has a significantly shorter duration. Normally this is not relevant, because the therapy starts after the hay-fever season and so the patients are not in a hurry. But there is one exception: there are a significant number of patients who visit the doctor shortly before the season starts. These patients are normally told to come back the following year, but with this product the doctor can start the therapy at the time of their visit. So the marketing department decided to position their product specifically to meet this occasion and it was a great success. The doctor did not have to switch the whole system (no behavioural costs), but was able to help the patient and earn additional revenue. In doing so he and his team became familiar with the new therapeutic scheme and this led them to prescribe this product even for those patients who didn't necessarily require such quick therapy.

Thinking in terms of situations and occasions, rather than individuals, can also be a springboard for innovations. Take the example of the fromage frais brand Frubes (see Figure 2.9).

Fromage frais is perceived to be healthy and natural, in part due to its link to milk. On which occasions might these characteristics be relevant? One occasion where healthy food is an important consideration is a child's lunch box. Mums want to ensure the best nutrition for their children and providing them with a lunch to take to school gives them a feeling of

Figure 2.9 Frubes' success is based on high added value through a perfect fit to a specific occasion

control over this. So fromage frais would be a good choice. From the brand's point of view the revenue potential from being used on this occasion is high due to its frequency. However, there are behavioural costs that are a barrier to usage: to eat the product from a traditional pot you need a spoon, and if the pot gets damaged in transit then the lunch box (and the child!) ends up in a mess. Frubes are a perfect fit for this occasion because the tube packaging enables the product to be consumed without a spoon and it's robust enough to not puncture or leak. The attitude towards fromage frais was positive before, but taking the situational context into account opened up a new opportunity worth many millions of pounds.

Purchase decisions are determined by the situational context as this shapes the perceived value and costs.

Besides using this perspective to help adapt our brands to fit certain usage occasions, we can also use it as a springboard to think of the decision-making process as a series of occasions. The task then is to consider how we can add value and/or reduce cost in the different steps along the purchase process. A good example comes from SMA, the world leader in producing power inverters for solar roof panels. Normally the only occasion on which they have contact with their clients (panel installers) is very late in the planning and purchase process for the panels. By looking at the complete purchase process SMA discovered an opportunity to add value and reduce cost for their clients. They developed an app called Solarchecker, which the installer can use when he is in early discussions with a house owner. He positions his smartphone on the roof, the app measures angles, calculates the expected productivity of the panels and, if fed with some more information, the craftsmen can tell the homeowner right away if it is worth buying solar panels or not. Once the app has calculated the productivity, the craftsmen can then order the appropriate power inverters directly from SMA. This app does not make the product better, but it increased the net value in favour of SMA.

What we have learned in this chapter

- The neuro-logic of a purchase decision is based on the equation: net value = reward – pain. The higher the net value, the more likely the purchase.
- In order to increase net value there are four strategic playgrounds which can all be used at the same time:
  1. Value (reward)
     a) Explicit value
     b) Implicit value
  2. Cost (pain)
     a) Explicit cost (financial)
     b) Implicit cost (behavioural)
- We need comparisons to make decisions. Value and cost are fundamentally relativistic.
- Since value and cost are relativistic, they can be significantly influenced by the situational context we are in.

What this means to us as marketers

- There need not be a trade-off between hard-selling and image-oriented marketing. In order to maximize net value, the same communication can highlight the value that the brand or service offers in combination with an attractive price message.
- The implicit level of cost allows us to maximize net value without actually reducing the price.
- Reducing behavioural costs can be a powerful lever to increase net value and thereby gain a competitive edge.
- Occasion-based marketing is a complementary perspective on consumer behaviour. It provides us with a springboard for innovation and offers strategic windows of opportunities.

3

Decoding the Interface

How the Autopilot Perceives Touchpoints

Perception is the door through which our marketing activities enter the mind of the consumer. Whether it's a promotional offer, product, pack, website or TV ad, perception of the signals that make up the interface between the brand and the consumer is the very first hurdle. This is why Kahneman integrates this key interface with the outside world into his decision-making framework. This chapter shows how perception works and how we can use the core insights to optimize our marketing activities.

The power of perception

Let's have a look at the following example to illustrate how powerful perception is and how it influences our decisions. Looking at Figure 3.1, which of the three women appears most attractive to men? And why?

About 70 per cent of all male respondents choose B (irrespective of the order in which the photos appear). But where does this dominant preference come from? What is the difference between the photos? The reason lies in the relationship between hips and waist size. All over the world, the most 'valued' ratio is 0.67. The further the ratio moves from this ideal, the less attractive it appears to men (A = 0.8 / C = 0.9). This shows the ability of the perceptual system to detect even the smallest differences and to base decisions on them. It demonstrates that even on the most automatic level, value is derived out of the most subtle signals.

The relevance to marketing of this direct link between perception and valuation is illustrated by the following example. Looking at the two bottle shapes in Figure 3.2: which holds more?

Most people anticipate that bottle A has the greater volume, and yet both bottles hold the same. Why is this? Priya Raghubir, Professor of Marketing at New York University, wanted to understand better which feature or element of a packaging format determines the volume perception of a

Figure 3.1 Which of the three women do men find most attractive?
Source: Shutterstock.com

Figure 3.2 Which bottle holds more?

product and, hence, influences the perception of value for money. She found that consumers use the height of a pack as the dominant signal and that perceptions of larger volumes based on elongation are associated with more purchases and increased consumption. Therefore, more vertically elongated packages may present a 'win-win' situation for brand managers; not only are they more likely to be purchased, but subsequently they also

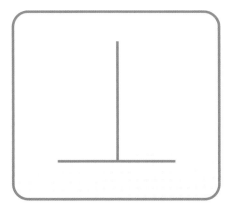

Figure 3.3 Actually these two lines are the same length despite how we perceive them

will be consumed at a faster rate. But why height and not depth or width? Let's look at Figure 3.3.

When we compare the two lines, the vertical line clearly appears longer than the horizontal line. But it's not – they are actually identical in length. So how come they don't appear to be? It's because our perception is not an exact 1:1 representation of the world. What we see is an interaction between the objective signal and the experiences stored in our memory and expectations derived from these memories. So why are vertically elongated packages perceived to contain more volume? We have implicitly learned that taller objects are often bigger (e.g. an elephant versus a mouse) and we transfer this rule of thumb to judge volume since bigger things have more volume. Therefore, in the case shown in the figure, bottle shape A is perceived to contain more volume because of its greater height – even though both bottles actually contain the same amount. If consumers explicitly think about it, they may mention depth as well, but in an automated decision-making mode, the implicit rule dominates the judgement.

One learning from this is that downsizing decisions (reducing volume while keeping price the same) must take volume perceptions into account.

Knowing the rules and mechanisms that determine what we perceive enables us as marketers to design our interfaces in an optimal way that matches these principles. If we had to choose between the packaging options pictured, then using the taller bottle is a way to increase volume perception – and therefore increase value perception.

There is a direct 'perception to action' link: perception can directly influence sales.

The eye is not a camera

We all know the saying 'seeing is believing', but we don't normally bother to even think about the importance of perception or how it works. Why would we? We get through the city traffic safely, so why bother? We don't wake up thinking, 'I must pay attention to perception today.' But, for us marketers, perception is crucial because it is the entry point for influencing purchase decisions. Because perception feels so natural and straightforward for us as human beings it's easy to assume that everything that we communicate to consumers will be perceived in exactly the way we intended. The case showing how volume impression changes depending on the shape of the bottle has already demonstrated, however, that the consumer's brain is not a passive but an active perceiver.

The following exercise demonstrates that our brain actively constructs that which we subjectively perceive. In Figure 3.4 you see a star on the left and a large dot on the right. Cover your left eye and look at the star using your right eye. With your left eye closed, slowly move closer to the book. At some point, the dot on the right will vanish (if you move even closer, it will re-appear).

Perception is an active process: our brain actively constructs what we perceive.

What is interesting is that your brain fills in the space where the dot was, in this case with the grey background colour. If your eye didn't see the dot, how did it see the grey background? It didn't – your brain made it up. If

Figure 3.4 The disappearing dot illusion

Figure 3.5 On the left, what we think we see. On the right, what we actually receive as input

the background were another colour, say green, then likewise your brain would complete the 'incomplete' picture using green.

So, how does our brain create our perception of the world? Let's start with the very first question: what 'picture' do our eyes send to the brain areas responsible for visual perception (interestingly, these areas sit in the back of our brain, despite our eyes being located in the front)? Figure 3.5 shows what happens. On the left-hand side is a picture of a street as we subjectively perceive it. We see everything in high resolution and full colour. This is our subjective view of the world: it feels as if we had a camera sitting on our eyes. However, the reality could not be more different.

The right-hand side shows the objective input into our brain. We see only a small part in sharp focus and in colour, and the rest becomes more and more blurred and loses more and more colour towards the periphery of our field of vision. The objective input consists of a small high-resolution sensor (the so-called fovea) as well as a low-resolution peripheral perception. The high-resolution sensor covers only a fraction of the overall input, roughly the size of a thumbnail. Everything else is blurred. What implications does that have?

Peripheral perception is key for maximizing the effectiveness of our marketing: through it the brain scans the environment to 'decide' what to focus on next. We want shoppers in supermarkets to be able to detect our brand via peripheral perception before they detect those of our competitors. This implies that we must use implicit signals to uniquely communicate the brand and the value it offers if we want consumers to focus their full attention on our products. For advertising, the implication is that if we can communicate the brand and its value, even through 'blurred' peripheral vision, then we will be much more effective since our ads will communicate even when a consumer's focus is on something else, e.g. on driving (for outdoor media) or on editorial content (for press and web advertising) – and not only will our ads still communicate, they will increase the likelihood of a consumer focusing on them in the first place.

Perception is based only on the blurred input from the periphery complemented by a small spot of high resolution.

Let's have a look at a retailer shelf through the lens of the autopilot (see Figure 3.6). The products are blurred. None of the text can be read, so no verbal messages follow. The cues we have to recognize and find the product, or the benefits, for which we are searching are mostly colours, shapes and sizes.

It's a useful (and often revealing) exercise to blur adverts, packaging designs, shelves or websites and ask ourselves what is perceivable in this

Figure 3.6 This is how consumers see a shelf via peripheral perception

'blurred mode'. Does the brand come through? How differentiated are we? What elements are perceivable at all? Is the small change we made to the logo perceivable? Does the packaging look different after the relaunch and, hence, is any newness really conveyed? We can answer these questions on the basis of expert judgement, but there are also ways to test them empirically. This can be done by defining different levels of blurring and to get test participants to recognize the product category, the brand and the key message as quickly as possible. If we include competitor ads or packaging we can create a map illustrating how our designs compare against an industry benchmark.

In one study where this was implemented for print adverts, ads from Garnier and Dove emerged as the most effective in communicating product and brand, even in highly blurred versions. These top-performing ads were able to communicate product and brand after an exposure of less than 100 milliseconds – this is less than one tenth of a second, or one quarter of the blink of an eye. This has obvious advantages when the average 'dwell time' on a print ad in a popular magazine has been shown to be less than two seconds.

The most common relaunches are tactical ones which involve only small changes to the packaging. Maybe the product's scent has a new name or a new benefit has been added. If the announcements of such changes are not perceivable through 'blurred vision', we should not expect any significant impact on sales. The relaunch may serve the purpose of giving the retailer the impression that we're still investing in the brand, but this will hardly have an impact on the consumer's perception of the product. The example shown in Figure 3.7 using the packaging of Dettol and Tesco antiseptic wipes shows that to our peripheral vision these two packs are very similar, which is beneficial for the private label but not for the branded product.

The shape is hard to distinguish; the dominant colours are white, blue and green. Both designs contain a swirling bluish element. The brand name is not legible. The distinctive signal is the round shape and the colour coding of the Dettol logo. Efficient recognition of the Dettol brand can only be based on these distinctive cues. A direct implication of this is that in communication – be it TV or displays – the distinctive cues of the packaging need to be present and prominent in order to build up a strong associative link between these cues, the brand and the message. Without this link, the recognition of our brand and product will be in danger. And even worse: if there is no perceivable and, hence, tangible difference between private-label and branded packaging, the perceived value added by the branded product is reduced, negating any potential brand advantage.

Effective and distinctive marketing communication needs to take the autopilot's perspective into account: messages need to be perceptible even in 'blurred vision' in order to be effective.

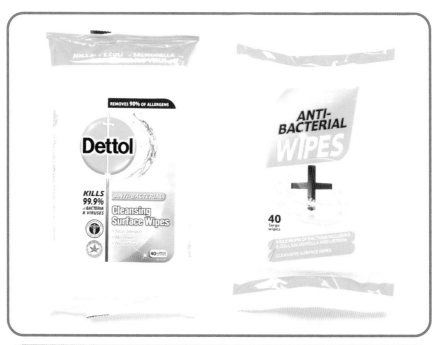

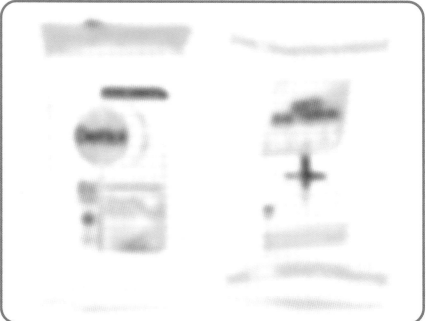

Figure 3.7 To be distinctive to the autopilot, packaging needs to be perceived differently through peripheral vision

Suggestion

Blur your packaging and advertisements. What is perceptible now? What do they communicate? What is distinctively recognizable? Brand, category, product, message?

Recognition – what is it?

We want consumers to find our product, we want our intended message to be perceived, and we want consumers to recognize our brand and our benefits. But how does that all work when our perception is based only on the blurred input from the periphery complemented by a small spot of high resolution? From the brain's perspective, in order to value a product it first needs to answer the question 'what is it?'. No matter whether it's a glass of wine, a car, a person or a product, we are not able to value things if we cannot recognize them. Recognition of products (and objects in general) happens very quickly (in less than the blink of an eye), is highly automatic and we have no explicit access to this process – it just happens. So, how does the brain recognize brands, products and messages?

Let's look again at the visual sense to illustrate the underlying mechanism (similar principles apply to the other senses but vision is especially important since it accounts for around 90 per cent of the 11 million bits per second that the autopilot processes). We have seen that the eye is not a camera, the brain does not get a picture as an input, and thus perception cannot be based on pictures. Figure 3.8 shows what really happens.

To the brain, to start with, products are nothing more than lines, edges, corners, curves, colours or movements. The brain disassembles a product

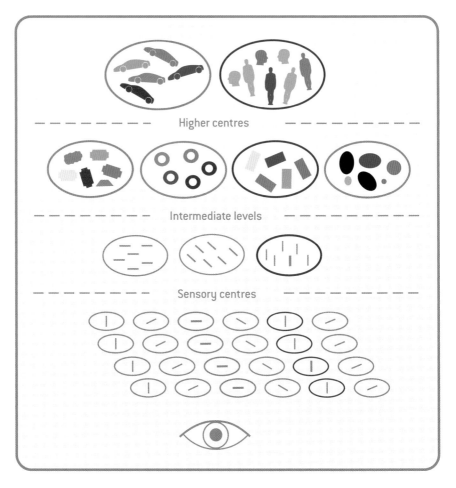

Figure 3.8 What we consciously perceive is an active construction based on different levels of processing in the brain

into its individual components, which are then, step by step, put together into a 'Gestalt' or overall pattern. To put it differently: the explicit and conscious perception of products is a construction that happens inside our head. Consciously, we may see a car, but to our brain, the car initially just consists of lines, edges, corners, curves and colours. Nothing else.

As our brain doesn't see images, it obviously doesn't store images either. There is no picture library inside the head. This allows our brain to be much more flexible. We can recognize a car as being a car even if we have never seen that model before or if it drives past in a new colour. After all, we want to recognize what it is – but we do not need to store every last detail to do so, as this would be terribly inefficient and would require enormous storage capacity. If we recognize things solely on the basis of previously stored images, we would all have had to have seen the exact same thing before. Every edge, every corner and every colour would have to be identical to what we have seen before. A small deviation, for instance a different colour, would make recognition impossible, as it would not be identical. Luckily, this is not the case. We recognize new models of cars as being cars, and can identify old friends even if we have not seen them for years and despite the fact that they will have changed (for example, more wrinkles, less hair or even grey hair). Fortunately, our flexibility to recognize in this manner also applies to products and brands, as Figure 3.9 shows.

Which brand is it? We have no problem recognizing that this represents Coca-Cola, despite having never seen this actual picture before and despite the fact that the logo has been changed significantly. So how does this recognition of the brand work? Our brain is built to be efficient but flexible at the same time. This is the reason why recognition is not based on each of the 11 million bits of input we receive from our senses. Rather,

Figure 3.9 The brand is clear despite the inaccuracy

79

recognition is based on those signals with the highest diagnostic value. For example, the constituent feature of a chair is that it has four legs and a back. If you take away the back from the chair it becomes a stool. It is only through this principle (constituent features having higher diagnostic value) that we are able to recognize old friends, even if we have not seen them for a long time, whether they are dressed differently or have a new hairstyle. The total picture can change significantly, but as long as the diagnostic cues are still there, we will be able to recognize it.

We have no picture memory. Our ability to recognize is based on signals with high diagnostic value.

Caricatures are a case in point: despite there being a lot of changes to the original, the main characteristics providing the dominant diagnostic cues are retained (say, Margaret Thatcher's hairstyle, teeth and nose), and so we have no problems recognizing the person.

For us as marketers that means, on the one hand, more freedom, but at the same time we have to be more conscious of what we do change. If we launch an exclusive line extension that we want to appear to be more premium, we might think of changing the colour of the logo from blue to gold or silver. If we assume that consumers store full pictures and use these for brand recognition, then this would be a non-starter. However, given what we have just learned about how the brain recognizes products and brands, we can start to discuss this topic more systematically. If the diagnostic value of colour is low for our brand, then consumers will have no problem recognizing it despite the change in colour. If, however, the brand's colour is important for recognition, as in the case of Coca-Cola, then we must not change it. While adjusting a logo may be problematic for internal reasons (e.g. it can be a signal for others to start tinkering with the Corporate Identity), the principle of diagnostic cues can be very helpful in deciding whether a specific signal such as a benefit visual, pack shape or background colour can be changed, or whether it would be better left unchanged.

The key is to know the diagnostic cues – beyond these we have a degree of freedom to change. What we should avoid at all costs is changing several of the key diagnostic cues simultaneously.

With this in mind let's take a look at the relaunch of Tropicana, the orange juice brand (see Figure 3.10). It caused some considerable attention in the marketing press when the newly introduced packaging – despite an advertising campaign worth millions – clocked up a loss of €30 million in just two months. Not surprisingly this led to the withdrawal of the new pack from sale.

The orange juice itself didn't change and tasted just as good as before. Likewise the brand name, and all it stood for, was consistent. Also, the new packaging certainly seems more modern (confirmed through market research) and may well look better on the breakfast table. However, in terms of recognition, the characteristics of the packaging have changed significantly: the symbol of the orange with a drinking straw stuck into it has been replaced by a glass; the font type has changed, as have the positions of all the main elements. The orange and the form of the logo of the previous design have a high diagnostic value for brand and product recognition. By changing these, automatic recognition, especially under conditions of low resolution (i.e. in peripheral vision), becomes almost impossible.

So knowing which signals and elements have high or low diagnostic value is crucial too when it comes to managing relaunches and pack design changes. But how can we clarify which these are? What constitutes the diagnostic value of a signal? Let's look at an example. Figure 3.11 shows products from different categories. Which are the light (low-calorie) products?

We have no problem answering this question. So, what constitutes a light product? Which characteristic has the highest diagnostic value? The

Before | After

Before | After

Figure 3.10 Tropicana changed several key diagnostic cues for brand recognition in the relaunch

Figure 3.11 One diagnostic cue for light products is a light blue colour

answer comes from comparing all light products and identifying what they all have in common. Which angles, colours, shapes, etc. do they share? In this case the answer is obvious: all the light products share the light blue colour. And this is exactly the principle that our brain uses when identifying the main diagnostic cues out of the enormous clutter of information. Based on associative learning, based on the principle of 'what fires together wires together', we learn that the probability is high that if a product uses a light blue in its packaging it is light product.

Whenever we get visual input from our receptors, our brain matches this information with whatever is stored in our associative memory. As soon as we find a sufficient overlap with stored diagnostic cues, recognition is complete. This process is completely implicit, and happens within milli-seconds. The reason that this happens so quickly is that our brain does not have to base the recognition on every piece of information but, instead, focuses on the main, and previously learned, diagnostic cues. If we needed to look at every last detail this would be terribly inefficient. We can assess the diagnostic power of each of our brand cues. This can be achieved by, for example, changing certain elements of our design and then testing its recognition performance. When main diagnostic cues are removed, the recognition will deteriorate. Another approach is to identify the main diagnostic cues in the category. By selectively removing brands from a typical shelf and asking participants to name the category as quickly as possible, we can identify which brand has the highest diagnostic value for a given category.

There are many ways to unlock diagnostic cues, but we should always make sure that we measure autopilot responses by getting participants to respond as quickly and as automatically as possible – without the pilot interfering.

Recognition is also based on contextual cues

Although the 'low saturated blue = light product' rule appears clear here, there is something missing. What if we see a car coloured like this? Or a shirt? Or shoes? We would hardly recognize these as light products, would we? Besides the diagnostic cues, there is another step required for efficient recognition. Take the case of accidentally bumping into a business partner we have been working with for ten years in a sauna or somewhere else where we haven't met him before. It takes us a while to recognize who it is and to categorize where we know this person from. The reason is that recognition is fundamentally context-sensitive. Think of a rose, a football or a house. It is hard to imagine seeing any of them without a background and/or other objects. Our experience from the visual world dictates our predictions about what other objects to expect in a scene, and their spatial configuration. Seeing a steering wheel inside a car sets expectations about where the radio, ashtray and mirrors might be. These predictable properties of our environment help us with object recognition. Recognizing someone's hand, for instance, significantly limits the possible interpretations of the object on that person's wrist to either a watch or a bracelet; it is not likely to be a belt or a tyre. So including the context in recognition is highly efficient.

Indeed, MIT neuroscientist Moshe Bar and his team found two working streams in the brain that, together, enable recognition. Recognition always requires two streams: one stream focuses on the object we are looking at and, in parallel, the other work stream processes information about the context we are in. Figure 3.12 shows how important context is for our brain to recognize an object. The hairdryer in the left panel and the drill in the right panel are visually identical objects: contextual information uniquely resolves ambiguity in each case. The context thus is equally important for recognition as the object itself.

Figure 3.12 Context determines whether it is a hairdryer (left panel) or a drill (right panel)

This means that we will often not recognize a person in places where we don't normally see them, because our memory not only stores the defining characteristics of that person but also stores the context in which we normally see them as a defining feature. This explains why we were so clear about the light products: the products we looked at were all food items and, specific to food categories, light products and low saturated blue is prototypical and therefore a diagnostic cue.

So recognition is driven by both the object and the context in which the object is placed. This provides us with an option to use context to influence the mental drawer in which consumers put our product. Unilever found that sales of their meat snack product, Peperami, rose significantly when it changed the location in retail stores where the product was sited. Previously, in the 1980s, they tried to capitalize on the benefits of the product being 'ambient-stable', i.e. it did not require refrigeration, to have the product placed alongside other snacks such as crisps. However, consumers did not expect a meat product to be anywhere other than in a chiller cabinet and so sales were somewhat suppressed. Given the in-store positioning context, at the time, the probability that this was a meat product was, simply, very low. When retailers re-sited the product alongside other chilled snacks, Peperami sales grew significantly.

The fact that recognition is context-sensitive also means that we don't need to cram so much information onto a pack design if we can use the environment in which the product is sold to provide recognition of what our product is. This also explains why people often remember having seen things in an advert that, objectively, are not there. One example is a toothbrush brand which for many years used a testimonial by an older man in its communications. They then replaced this testimonial using a younger, female presenter instead. Even though the difference between a younger female presenter and an older male is seemingly obvious, more than half of the respondents in research recalled seeing the male testimonial when in fact they had seen ads that featured only the female presenter. This happens because the brand acts as the context within which the story is received. The male testimonial was wired into each respondent's neural network of this brand, and was activated whenever the brand was recognized. The other details of the ad were then overshadowed by the expectation of seeing the male testimonial.

The autopilot uses both diagnostic codes and the context to recognize brands and products.

Concepts – what does it stand for?

The multinational beer company Anheuser-Busch InBev has a German beer brand in its portfolio: Hasseröder (see Figure 3.13). This brand recently invested €30 million to update their 0.5 litre bottle. What they changed was the neck of the bottle: from a round cross section to a hexagon. The beer itself was not altered.

In order to increase sales, this change must increase the perceived value of the product. But why should the cross section of the neck of the bottle

Figure 3.13 The German beer brand Hasseröder introduced a new bottle neck shape

change the perceived value? The question 'what is it' which we covered earlier is not sufficient to answer this because it is still the same brand, still the same logo and still the same product. To understand the process by which such changes can impact the perceived valuation and thus sales, let's first have a look at a fascinating study conducted by Christof Koch from California Institute of Technology. Koch and his research team used epileptic patients for an unusual experiment. These patients had electrodes implanted in their brains in order to locate the epilepsy centre. The researchers then showed them pictures of celebrities, from Bart Simpson to Bill Gates to Halle Berry. The result? For each celebrity a different set of neurons lit up. The more fascinating result was that the 'Halle Barry-neurons' were activated regardless of whether she was viewed from the left or the right, with or without a hat or sunglasses, smiling or not, with or without the Cat Woman costume or even when only the words 'Halle Berry' were shown. In all of these situations the same neurons fired. What does that mean? This demonstrates that it is not important to the brain how the brand Halle Berry is encoded, whether as an image or merely as text; as long as the *meaning* of 'Halle Berry' is recognizable, the neurons fire. Our brain not only answers the question 'what is it?' but in addition decodes what a signal means, what it stands for. This is why we can recognize the O2 brand based on only the bubbles and the blue background. Therefore the second major question the brain 'asks' when perceiving something is: 'What does it stand for?' Let's have a closer look at this crucial second step in decoding brands and products.

Imagine you are invited to the birthday party of one of your work colleagues and as a present you bring her a bouquet of roses. Merely imagining this right now probably makes us feel uncomfortable. But why? A rose is a flower, it looks nice, it smells good, etc. It is just as nice as a sunflower, in fact, but the reaction of the recipient (and of those witnessing the gift) will certainly be very different. The reason why we feel uncomfortable with roses as a gift, but not sunflowers, is the meaning they convey in this

Figure 3.14 The two flowers activate different mental concepts. In our culture a sunflower stands for happiness and a rose for romance

context. Roses stand for – at least in our culture – romance and love. A sunflower, in contrast, stands for happiness (see Figure 3.14). They mean different things and this meaning determines the perceived value in a given context. If your colleague is in love with you, the perceived value will be high, whereas if she is happily married, to give her the roses will cause some embarrassment at the very least.

In ancient times we competed to be the alpha male, the leader of the pack, by fighting. Today we do the same but in more flexible, and less painful, ways. Hierarchies in companies are symbolically encoded by the distance between a designated car-parking space and the entrance, the size of desk or offices, where the boss sits in meeting rooms or who speaks most often in a meeting. We are able not only to say 'I love you' with words but also to meaningfully express it through the giving of a rose or a diamond ring. We prepare soup to care for someone who's ill, or make coffee to socialize. Only humans can intuitively understand that a cool blue has something to do with achievement and a warm blue with nurturing and care. The way in which we're able to do this is something that is uniquely human. While we share many characteristics with animals, such as emotion, curiosity and social behaviour, the capability to translate signals to something more abstract, into a mental concept, is specific to us humans. In a scientific paper published in the *Annual Review of Psychology*, well-known behavioural economist Dan Ariely refers to this as 'conceptual consumption':

> *Our prehistoric ancestors spent much of their waking hours foraging for and consuming food, an instinct that obviously paid off. Today this instinct is no less powerful, but for billions of us it's satisfied in the minutes it takes to swing by the store and pop a meal in the microwave. With our physical needs sated and time on our hands, increasingly we're finding psychological outlets for this drive, by seeking out and consuming concepts.*

Signals we send – from colours to shapes to brand logos – are recoded into mental concepts based on learned associations in memory. Perceived value is based on the mental concepts triggered by brand and product. Purchase decisions are based on these mental concepts, and not on the signals as such.

What happens in the brain is this: after we have recognized what an object is, this information is translated into a mental concept where additional meaning is applied. We see the rose, we recognize it is a rose and then our associative memory activates prototypical things we have already learned about roses, such as typical occasions where we came across a rose. By this process, we apply meaning. The SUV (sport utility vehicle) in the driveway is only partly about the need for transport; the concept consumed is that of social status. Dozens of studies have teased out the many ways in which such concepts can influence people's purchase or consumption, over and above the physical product itself. One could say we turn a physical object X into a mental concept Y, e.g. a bouquet of roses into the concept of love, or the SUV into the concept of status. This 'X equals Y' transformation is called recoding (e.g. SUV = status). Visual elements such as shape, colour, logo and typeface are perceived not only in terms of their formal or technical properties but also in terms of the mental concepts they trigger.

Rounded logos, for example, are generally perceived as more harmonious and less aggressive than angular logos. Likewise, studies have demonstrated a relation between a product's relative height and perceived dominance. This finding can be explained in experiential terms – being in a high position is associated with greater control (e.g. visual control over those below) or power (e.g. objects are easier to manipulate from above). Because we've experienced the association between vertical interaction and concepts such as dominance, pride or control in our everyday lives, we find that variations in relative height influence the extent to which products are perceived as expressive of those related concepts (e.g. pride or dominance).

A case in point is a company selling big cranes for the construction industry. Their advertising is used to communicate facts and advantages of the vehicles, their performance parameters and much more. In order to make the ad stand out, the agency showed close-ups of the cranes. No people can be seen. The advert fails. An analysis shows that the problem lies in the crane operator's fear of the gigantic crane's superiority. This invalidates all the factual arguments designed for the explicit system, the pilot. Hence, the way the cranes were portrayed in the advertising implicitly carried a message which the client had not intended at all. The crane operator's autopilot appears to have decoded a very different message: 'The crane is stronger than you.' For this advert to work we would need to convince the crane driver's autopilot that it will take him only a few hand movements to 'command' the crane and take control of it. Optimizing the advert is not about simply putting a person in it, it must show how the crane operator has control over the crane.

Recoding: From signals to concepts

Recoding means that sensory and motor input is translated into mental concepts. How this works on a neuronal level is shown by Figure 3.15 by Joaquin Fuster, a leading neuroscientist at the University of California.

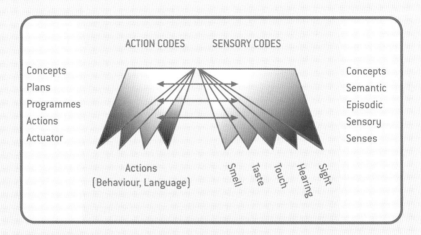

Figure 3.15 Everything we perceive and do is recoded to mental concepts

As the figure shows, there are two main strands in the brain: one from the senses to the brain and one from our actions (e.g. finger movements) to the brain. Right at the 'top' are the mental concepts as the highest level, which nonetheless are directly connected to the levels that lie below, i.e. there is a systematic and non-arbitrary link between signals and concepts. This is why seeing a red rose triggers concepts such as 'love' or an SUV is linked with status.

Insights into the structural relationships between visual elements and symbolic meanings are important, not least because a considerable number of studies have demonstrated the increasing importance of mental concepts with respect to consumer decision making and the formation of brand impressions. According to this line of research, the most important function of a product's appearance for consumers, apart from bringing aesthetic pleasure, is the portrayal of mental concepts. One implication of this that we will come back to later in this book is that we should not judge visuals, colours, font types, shapes or testimonials on the basis of whether something is aesthetically pleasing (i.e. whether we like it). Rather, we should follow the process that the brain employs and ask what the signal stands for, and which concept it triggers.

A significant advantage of neuroscience and modern psychological science is that they provide us with a quantitative and analytical approach to this intangible layer of meaning. One such approach is a dedicated neuronal marker (known as N400) to establish whether or not there is a semantic fit between a signal (e.g. a key visual) and a given concept (e.g. 'performance') – without having to explicitly ask people (which would engage the pilot instead of engendering an autopilot response). Whenever the brain recognizes a semantic fit between a signal and a concept there's a change in neuronal activity in specific parts of the brain, in particular the frontal and lateral neocortex. This change in activity can be measured via EEG and is visible from studying what scientists call the 'evoked potential' after c.400 milliseconds.

Neuronal markers of semantic fit are interesting, but often not very practical when it comes to measuring representative samples in various cities or even countries, or linking them with existing metrics from surveys such as recall or purchase intention. Fortunately, there are additional, more practical ways to measure which concepts a signal triggers, such as the so-called priming techniques from psychological sciences. Thanks to advances in technology, especially the ability to measure spontaneous

What signals stand for, and which concepts they trigger, can be measured objectively using quantitative tools from neuroscience and psychology. These tools measure the implicit associations between signals and mental concepts.

responses to signals, we do not have to resort to subjective judgement and opinion or neuronal markers to derive an analytical assessment of the all-important mental concepts triggered by signals we use in marketing. One of the biggest advantages of quantitative assessments is to be able to compare implicit associations across countries and cultures. While it may be possible to unlock implicit meanings within a given culture, it is much harder to compare the results across cultures. This is where an objective, quantitative measure can really add value.

Now, coming back to the case of the hexagon bottle neck of the Hasseröder relaunch: what does it stand for? Is it just a gimmick or is there more to it? What is the meaning, the mental concept, that is activated when we perceive this feature? The form is angled and rugged, hence less smooth than the standard round shape. Research shows that shape angularity influences perceptions of product potency. For instance, straight, angular forms are generally perceived as stronger and more masculine than rounded, curved forms, which are generally perceived as more gentle, soft or feminine.

So, overall, compared with a round-shaped neck, the hexagon neck is more masculine and this form strengthens the perception of the brand as masculine. Given the brand's claim 'Because men know why', this change fits the positioning and increases the perceived value among beer drinkers for whom masculinity is rewarding. The consumer buys the concept of masculinity with this beer. In one study by researchers from the University of Twente in the Netherlands, it was shown that if the shape (natural versus artificial) of a water bottle matches the concept conveyed by an advertising slogan, then both the product and the brand evaluation are positively affected. Knowing this, there is an additional benefit of the conceptual congruence between the Hasseröder brand claim and the new bottle neck shape.

Figure 3.16 The new packaging design conveys different concepts and therefore different value compared with the original design

Looking at the Tropicana packaging again (see Figure 3.16), and now applying this process, shows not only that the new design was a barrier for efficient recognition but that the concept, the meaning, triggered by the design has changed significantly.

The main visual on the new pack is a glass of orange juice. Where do we prototypically see this type of glass in our everyday life? When do we see it? Relatively rarely. It's unlikely that there are many families where this sort of glass would feature on the breakfast table every morning. For those families, what does that say about them? What prototypical family does that correspond to? Rather wealthy and well-to-do. When have we used such a glass? In a hotel perhaps, or when invited to a celebration. Maybe when we've invited friends over for dinner. All of these experiences activate the concept of 'special occasion', so what does that say about the occasions for which this product is suitable?

Let's now look at the original design. Naturally, the orange communicates what it is – an orange juice – but also much more besides. There's a leaf next to it. Where is something like this familiar from? Actually, only from oranges that have just been picked. So this activates the concept of freshness. The glass doesn't do that. With a glass we don't know whether the juice is fresh or not. It could be fresh, but there is no perceptible signal to say this and, as we know by now, the associative memory can't be automatically activated without a perceptible signal. What associations do we have with the straw in our memory? What sort of straw is it? A cocktail straw? Hardly, because it has coloured rings around it and that's the kind of straw we give to our children – so it's a straw for everyday use. All in all, not only does the question 'what is it?' (recognition) appear problematic but the meaning conveyed by the new design has fundamentally changed.

The objective was to show more 'premiumness'. That was achieved as the new design is certainly more refined, but whether the associated concept motivated consumers has to be doubted given the dramatic fall in sales. For us as marketers this conceptual level is key to managing and boosting the value perception of our products.

As with recognition, meaning is context-sensitive. In marketing we spend lots of time discussing which signals to use in a TV commercial or on a pack. However, we tend to evaluate, the key visual for example, without taking the context systematically into consideration. Figure 3.17 shows that this distracts us from having efficient and more objective discussions because meaning, just like perception and memory, is context dependent.

If we read these as two separate lines, we all most probably decode the signal in the middle on the upper line as a 'B' and on the lower line as '13' despite them being identical. Clearly, the context defines which meaning comes through. Imagine you want to use a diamond as a symbol in communication. A diamond is associated with more than one meaning.

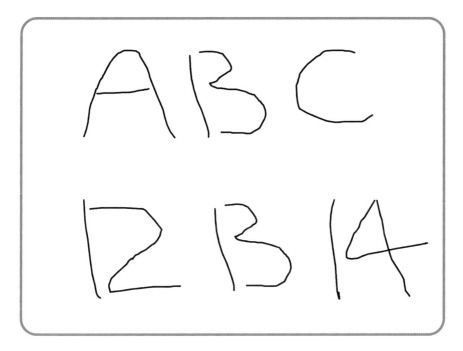

Figure 3.17 Meaning is context dependent

It can stand for robustness, for brilliance, for luxury, for marriage. Which of those meanings will be perceived by the consumer depends on the context in which it is presented. If you put a diamond in an ad about construction instruments then robustness will most likely be the dominant meaning. If, however, you put it on a pack containing hair colourant, it is likely to activate the concept of brilliance. Therefore taking the context into consideration when discussing executions will make our discussions more effective.

Meaning is context dependent.

New and consistent – squaring the circle?

There are many ways to express concepts such as status or love. The rose is only one way to signal love or romance. A ring or a heart with an arrow can convey the same mental concept. This flexibility of the human brain to associate different signals with the same concept offers the possibility to overcome one of the major dilemmas we face in brand management: the trade-off between newness and consistency. We all recognize these two demands – to be new and yet at the same time consistent. We want to change something because we want to grow sales and brand share, to offer new incentives or win back customers. At the same time, we want to maintain our current and historic strengths and hence still be recognizable and consistent, not risking the alienation of any existing customers. There are good reasons for being consistent, but there are also good reasons for newness. Little wonder, then, that we have many discussions on this very topic – what must we keep constant and what can, or indeed should, we change?

Cognitive psychologists have known for a long time that our brain learns best when we can integrate new knowledge into pre-existing knowledge. Therefore, familiarity is very important for advertising effectiveness and efficiency. That much we know. But why do we humans often find it so hard to learn new things? It is down to the way the brain responds to stimulation. Researchers at the Radboud University in Nijmegen (Netherlands) measured the activity of nerve cells reacting to familiar and new – i.e. unexpected – information. If a signal was expected – i.e. it was consistent with expectations – then this information was not processed further. Information that matches expectation is suppressed. Cells switch off or deal with other things. This neuronal switching-off effect is one reason why most car crashes happen on roads that we know best. We no longer concentrate enough and our brain completes the information from memory. As soon as we expect something and our hypothesis is confirmed by a signal, our brain switches off and attends to other matters. This is very efficient. Why should we spend more time considering something when we already know what it is? This is why communication has to be sufficiently new in order for consumer learning to be achieved. In other words, without newness only existing associations will be activated, and nothing is learned. Newness opens the door for new things to be communicated.

The way out of the dilemma between consistency and newness is the distinction between the perceivable signals and the concepts they trigger through recoding. In order to make use of both consistency and newness, we need to be consistent at the meaning level, but new at the signal level. The Hasseröder bottle is a case in point. The angular-shaped bottle neck is a new signal, but it fits and even strengthens the concept of masculinity and hence increases perceived value in the context of the overall brand promise 'Because men know why'. Another good example of how this can be managed is Lynx/Axe (see Figure 3.18). This brand is very consistent at the conceptual level but uses a translation of its proposition every time anew. In every TV ad the average guy gets the most beautiful girls, which of course has high perceived value, especially for young adults, but this mechanism is translated in many ways. What is particularly important is that, in all of the brand's campaigns, the specific product and its properties are connected to the overall brand promise. By doing this, familiarity at a brand or message level is achieved and the specific product is linked to it.

The way out of the dilemma between consistency and newness is to be consistent at the meaning level, but new at the signal level.

Figure 3.18 Lynx/Axe: new signals but always the same meaning

But how much newness can the consumer cope with? How much familiarity is necessary? 'Disruptive' communication, which goes completely against expectations, does create attention and higher cognitive activity – consumers try to solve the inconsistency – but can be kept up long term only in exceptional cases and this requires the recipient to be highly involved. Advertising, however, is usually processed with low involvement (and advertising researchers are in agreement on this). Research shows that the most effective strategy to utilize is the MAYA principle: Most Advanced Yet Acceptable. Many studies agree that a message that is moderately incongruent with expectations is the most efficient at increasing attention, liking, recall and recognition. Being consistent at the meaning level and new on the signal level is one way to implement the MAYA principle.

The MAYA principle: a moderate degree of newness, in combination with some familiarity, is the most effective for marketing communication.

Value-based attention: What we want is what we see

We have now seen how the first step in the decision-making process unfolds: how the brain recognizes products and brands, and how it recodes signals into concepts, using the context within which the signals are perceived. One key question remains though: how do we allocate attention to signals? What determines whether we pay attention to this or that product, advert or pack design? What most of us experience is the fact that we recognize some things more often than others and this varies over time. When we become a parent, for example, we suddenly notice more children and babies around than we ever did before. If we are interested in buying a certain car we suddenly see this particular car all over the place; and not just the car itself, but advertisements for it as well. Indeed, research shows that we notice the corresponding advertisements more *after* we've decided to buy a particular car.

So when developing communication we need to be aware that our current customer base will be paying the most attention to it. What is the underlying mechanism for these effects? How do they work? This leads us to one of the most talked-about topics in marketing and advertising: attention. When it comes to how our message, brand or products get into the heads of consumers, the first thing that often comes to mind is attention. We need an attention-grabbing campaign! We need more impact on shelf! We need to cut through the clutter! Such requirements and objectives will be familiar to all marketers. Let's see what science can tell us about how attention works.

We have already seen that we have two kinds of perception, peripheral and focal. Now, in order for us to see as much of the world as clearly as possible, it's pretty obvious that we have to move our eyes. In so doing, our focal attention moves. But how does that happen? How do we decide where to look first and where to look next? Since we make these kind of decisions 2–3 times a second (allowing for sleep, this works out at about 150,000 times per day), and given that we are not aware of these eye movements, these decisions cannot be based on a conscious, controlled decision process but, rather, on an implicit, automatic one. So what is the key principle by which we decide where to direct our small, high-resolution sensor and, therefore, whether we see a product or advertisement in full focus? Again, it comes back to the basic principle of decision making: it is based on value.

Research conducted by an outdoor marketing company found that three times as many wine drinkers looked at outdoor advertising for wine than beer drinkers did (measured via eye tracking). Our first reaction may well be so what? Why shouldn't a wine drinker look at wine? But a second look at this finding prompts an important question: what raised the wine drinkers' propensity to look at wine advertising *before* they actually looked at it? It wasn't a case of wine drinkers looking at wine advertising for longer than beer drinkers do, nor did their broad gaze return to the advertising more often – the key point, and what is so amazing, is that three times more wine drinkers directed their focal perception to it.

So what triggers that first look? The answer is based on what we've just learned – that we have two kinds of attention: a peripheral, implicit attention and a focal, explicit attention. And this is how it works. The incoming peripheral signals are processed implicitly by the autopilot. It scans the environment with a much broader scope (of the 11 million bits of data that the autopilot processes, about 90 per cent is received visually) and processes all of the incoming information. Information about an object (e.g. brand logos, an outdoor ad or a TV ad) is instantly propagated to the brain region that we encountered in the previous chapter: the reward, or value, centre (OFC). Activation in this reward centre has been observed between 80 and 130 ms after stimulus onset, which is less than the blink of an eye. The point of this process is to evaluate, early on, the value of what we perceive.

Like a value scout, the autopilot constantly evaluates everything we perceive and if whatever is received matches our needs, desires and goals then the autopilot assigns a high value to it. If the value is high, then our focal attention is directed to this signal by 'telling' the eye muscles to move towards it. Moshe Bar, the MIT neuroscientist we met earlier in this chapter, summarizes this process as follows:

> *Responses signalling an object's salience, relevance or value do not occur as a separate step after the object is identified. Instead, affective responses support vision from the very moment that visual stimulation begins.*

Therefore the brain not only recognizes an object at lightning speed, it also evaluates its value within a fraction of a second – and this valuation then determines where our eyes and, hence, our focal attention will move. As the photographs in Figure 3.19 show, if we're hungry, our autopilot scans

Figure 3.19 Attention is driven by what we value at that given time. The bottom two figures show eye-tracking results for study participants who were hungry (lower left panel) or satiated after lunch (lower right panel). Hungry participants focused on the McDonald's logo, while the satiated group allocated more attention to the shop windows and logos

the environment and directs our focal perception to the signals that promise to fit with our goals: in this case towards the McDonald's sign. If we are looking for shoes, our focal attention is guided towards other signals such as the shop windows. In other words: value drives attention.

This means that relevance is a key driver of attention: we see what we want. The basic point is that we need to signal the value that people are looking for in a way that the autopilot can detect and perceive.

Many studies show that our current goals guide the automatic allocation of our attention. Looking for a can of Coke will enhance processing of red areas in our visual input by increasing the neuronal sensitivity for that particular colour. Therefore, red cans will be seen with higher attention and thus noticed more quickly compared with, for example, blue cans. With this in mind let's have another look at the detergent shelf (see Figure 3.20).

The consumer's autopilot will search for signals that 'tell' them, based on input which is mostly blurred, which of these packs most probably fits their goals best. If they want a detergent specifically for washing black clothes, which pack signals this benefit most strongly and why? The one that best signals to the autopilot that it is the right choice in this respect will then get attention. What would you look for if you want a detergent that cares specifically for woollens? Most probably at those packs coloured pink. In France a wool detergent brand changed its pink colour to a creamy white in order to increase the 'caring' proposition of the product. Sales dropped and most lapsed users went to a pink-coloured competitor. The same is true if consumers are looking for specific brands. Where would you look if you were searching for Ariel? Most probably at those green packs with a vague red, angled element in the middle.

In order to attract attention, signals that brands and products send should fit with consumer goals. Attention is more 'pull' than 'push'. People 'let our message in' if there is a match with their goals.

Figure 3.20 In order to attract attention, signals that products send should fit with consumer goals

The autopilot is the gatekeeper for our marketing messages. It opens the door for our messages, offers, products and brands only if their perceived value is high enough. Even the gaudiest nursery with the trendiest of concepts will not be able to find an activated goal with which to connect with a 20-year-old single man. This is why he might register the nursery implicitly, but none of it will have any effect on him or affect his behaviour. There is one thing that is important to recognize here: people cannot be manipulated at will. Simply show them a few nice pictures and they will dutifully march off to the shops and buy our brand? Of course it doesn't work like this. We cannot be manipulated if we don't want to be. If something is not compatible with our implicit or explicit goals (at that moment and in that context), we won't do it. Not only that, we won't even perceive it.

Figure 3.21 Attention is also driven by contrast

The 'pop-out' effect – attention is also triggered by contrast

The mechanisms we just described are driven by value: our attention serves what is important to us; it serves our goals and needs. However, there is a purely signal-based attention path as well. Figure 3.21 shows how this mechanism works.

Search for the 'Q' and the 'F' in the figure. For most people it's easy to see the Q, but finding the F is much harder (12th in row 6). Both are different letters to E, but Q stands out because the visual contrast with E is higher; the shapes are clearly different. Our visual system is highly tuned to detect and focus on contrasts – without contrast we cannot separate the object from the background. This was crucial 50,000 years ago to separate the tiger's face from the surrounding woods.

So if we want to stand out from the surroundings, or if we want to direct attention towards our product, we have to manage the degree of perceptible contrast. This is exactly what we have in mind when we say we want to 'cut through' advertising clutter or to achieve 'stand-out' on shelf. We want to grab focal attention by disruption, by being different and by standing out. However, merely getting attention won't make people buy. Let's assume that E, F and Q are products. If someone is searching for an F, then recognizing the Q, simply because it stands out, will not make him buy it if it does not meet a current goal.

A good example of integrating 'pull' and 'push' strategies is Vanish, the stain remover (see Figure 3.22): it creates a pop-out effect by using a vibrant, fluorescent colour. Importantly, the colour (pink) fits the core

Figure 3.22 Which colour fits 'powerful stain removal' best?

benefit of this category, i.e. 'strong cleaning performance'. Using yellow would also have been striking, but would not have fitted with the consumer's goals. Why not? Which colour would you use to convey powerful stain removal, pink or yellow? In most countries the Vanish colour is associated with the concept of strength, and this is certainly beneficial for a stain-removal product.

Perceptual fluency adds value

Look at the two pictures of a piece of cake in Figure 3.23. These were tested as part of a study by Marketing Professors Ryan Elder and Aradhna Krishna to see which one would have the highest purchase intent. Which one do you think did?

If you thought the one on the right then you're correct: compared with the picture on the left it resulted in a 20 per cent uplift in purchase intention (for right-handed participants). But why? The only difference is the orientation of the fork. Why should something seemingly so trivial actually affect our behaviour? Simply because it's a better fit to what we

Figure 3.23 Where the fork is placed impacts persuasion.
Reproduced by permission of Ryan Elder. Sourced from 'The "Visual Depiction Effect" in Advertising' (2011)

normally perceive (if we are right-handed). This, as such, is of value for the autopilot because it is easier to process. Scientists refer to this as perceptual fluency because what we are familiar with requires less effort to process and is therefore valued more highly by the autopilot.

For marketing, perceptual fluency is a driver to attract attention and to provide value for customers. A consumer can see a TV ad one night and implicitly learn a certain icon from that ad. Upon seeing the same icon on a retail shelf the next day, having seen it previously makes it easier to process this information. The perceptual cost is reduced and this increased fluency makes the difference. This effect can help especially in categories where the perceived values of products and brands are very similar. For this to work, the visual, perceptible link between the TV ad, the packaging and the POS is crucial. Quite often we have one team dealing with above-the-line communication and another team dealing with POS communication. The result is that many key visuals we use at the POS are not optimally linked with the TV campaigns and so the fluency effect is not fully exploited.

In order to exploit fluency we need to perceivably link broadcast media campaigns (e.g. TV) and POS communication.

A good indication that fluency is at work is the following situation. Whenever a campaign is launched, sales go up, but as soon as the campaign stops, sales return back to baseline. This indicates that sales were driven by fluency: the campaign made the brand mentally more fluent, which resulted in an increase in the ease of processing that brand at the POS.

An example of a recent campaign that made the brand more fluent is the successful 'Sandwich' campaign from Walkers, helping to sell an extra 15.6 million packets of crisps. This dramatized the creative idea that Walkers 'makes any sandwich more exciting' by bringing celebrities such as Pamela Anderson, Jenson Button and Marco Pierre White to the town of Sandwich in Kent and surprising the residents there, making the town itself more exciting. This campaign increased the mental availability of the

Automatically	AUTOMATICALLY
Insurance documents	INSURANCE DOCUMENTS
Cauliflowers	CAULIFLOWERS
Celebrations	CELEBRATIONS

Figure 3.24 Capital letters are harder to read

brand and hence its fluency, and specifically in the context of sandwiches. At the POS the product was placed next to the sandwich section, which further increased and exploited this fluency based on the conceptual fit to the campaign.

Another aspect of fluency, in the sense of ease and efficiency of processing, is how words are perceived. Often we see information written in capital letters (see Figure 3.24) mostly for aesthetic reasons (or to achieve stand out). Unfortunately science shows that this creates a barrier for the auto-pilot to process the information.

The reason is that when we learn to read we start by reading every single letter and then we put the word together. As we know from watching or helping children, this is a slow process. As always, with repetition, the autopilot takes over and applies more efficient rules that are based on experience and memory. The recognition of words is no longer based on perceiving every single letter but, rather, on using the form or shape of the word as additional information. This enables us to read very quickly. However, if a word is presented in capital letters, then the learned word form cannot be used. This forces our brain to behave as if we had just learned to read: we have to read letter by letter. Consequently, this makes reading relatively slow. Capital letters might look nice, and we might think that they add impact, but they are less fluent, and therefore less effective if the message we send out relies on efficient perception – for example in packaging, posters or TV advertising.

Faces are of high value

In marketing one of the most common visual cues in all of advertising is the human face. Indeed, faces have a special value for the human brain. Seeing a (good-looking) face triggers the reward centre in the brain. Not only that, there is a brain region dedicated to the recognition of faces. This brain region (fusiform gyrus) lights up every time we see faces, including in advertising. The facial area is highly specialized. However, there are certain areas of perception, for which it is used as well, because these areas have face-like features, such as animals, cartoons, the famous smiley :-) or the Thomson Holidays/TUI brand logo. All these things signify 'face' from the brain's perspective, even if they resemble a human face, at best, remotely. The 'face' of a car with the headlights for eyes and a smiling radiator grille activates the facial area for this same reason.

Since faces are rewarding we tend to look at them automatically. So whenever we use a face in an ad it is safe to assume that attention will go there early on. What is even more interesting is the so-called 'joint attention' effect: we tend to look in the direction where another face is looking. We all are familiar with the situation of five people looking up into the sky which results in more people stopping and looking in the same direction – even though there is nothing special to be seen. The tendency to look where others are looking makes sense from an evolutionary standpoint: one individual alerts another to an object (e.g. a lion) by means of eye-gaze. This effect can be exploited to guide attention. This was shown in a pretest where the same ad triggered a higher purchase intention if the female in the ad looked at the product compared with when she looked straight ahead. A beer promotion using a picture of a celebrity triggered much higher sales if the celebrity gazed in the direction of the beer rather than elsewhere.

Since we have way more than 10,000 hours of experience of processing faces it does not come as a big surprise that facial recognition is an automatic, implicit process. In one study, subtly (and imperceptibly) incorporating elements of an individual's face into an otherwise unfamiliar face, through digital manipulation called 'morphing', increased that individual's level of reported trust in, and preference for, the unfamiliar face. In a fascinating experiment by Robin Tanner from Wisconsin School of Business, digitally blending an unfamiliar face with 35 per cent of the face of Tiger Woods resulted in a composite face that was perceived as more trustworthy than the original face before the Tiger Woods scandal, and the effect reversed after his reputation was damaged. This effect occurred despite 100 per cent of participants failing to identify any resemblance between the Tiger-morphed face and Tiger Woods himself (see Figure 3.25).

The origin of these effects is familiarity: to the autopilot, the morphed-in face of a celebrity is more familiar and hence can be trusted more, even if we do not even detect the celebrity consciously with the pilot system. One suggestion emerging from this effect is, rather than placing celebrities and highly familiar figures front and centre as brand endorsers, to utilize them (or, even better, look-alikes) to subtly morph their faces with those of otherwise unfamiliar stock model images.

Indeed, such a strategy may even have the potential to outperform explicit use of celebrities in some circumstances. Research has demonstrated that the persuasive impact of spokespersons can be enhanced when their prior exposure cannot be recalled, as this recollection would facilitate misattribution of the perceptual fluency experienced while processing the endorser. Put differently, when the endorser is correctly identified, any

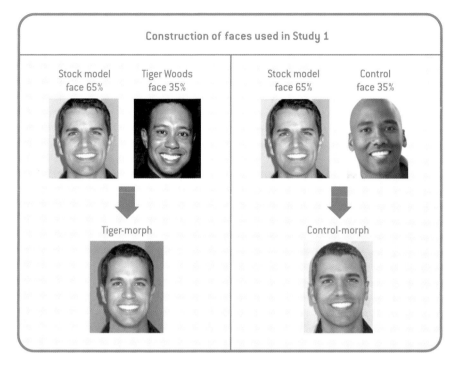

Figure 3.25 Familiarity works at an implicit level
Reproduced by permission of Robin Tanner. Sourced from his paper 'A tiger and a president: imperceptible celebrity facial cues influence trust and preference', *Journal of Consumer Research*, December 2012

effect of fluency is more likely to be correctly attributed to their fame and familiarity, rather than to the brand or the product.

Price sensor – the sixth sense

We conclude this chapter on perception with a sixth sense: the price sense. It turns out that our brain processes prices using very similar principles as when seeing, hearing or touching. Most importantly, price perception is influenced, like all our senses, by context and is therefore fundamentally relativistic. In the previous chapter we saw that perceived cost can be reduced by contextual signals such as a promotional flash. That the graphical representation of a price has an influence on its perception is easy to understand. However, does the distance, or spacing, between two prices matter? This was the question that a study by pricing researcher Keith Coulter in the *Journal of Consumer Psychology* looked into. The result? The greater the physical horizontal distance between a reference price and a discount price, the greater the perceived difference between the two prices (see Figure 3.26). The perceived price discount increases with physical distance and, with it, the attractiveness of the discount and hence an increased probability of purchase.

We perceive numbers more readily and easily in the horizontal plane than vertically. We learned to read and to process numbers like this and it's the reason why a gesture for big and small is often encoded by the horizontal distance between our hands: if we want to illustrate a huge number, we increase the distance between our hands, almost as if we were stretching something.

Psychological studies show that numbers exist along a mental number line, with the larger entries on the right and smaller entries on the left (see Figure 3.27). It becomes increasingly difficult to discriminate among two places on a number line as the distance between the two places decreases. The higher the numbers, the more closely they 'stay together'. This is known as the Weber–Fechner law and is important in areas of all magnitude estimation, including the evaluation of prices and discounts.

The key insight is that the way in which price is presented is, in itself, a powerful lever, without even having to change the actual price, let alone the product. A lot is known about how people represent and process numbers, including prices, and we can use this knowledge to optimize price perception rather than lower actual prices.

So if we're faced with high costs of hundreds or thousands of pounds – such as buying a car, or a builder's quotation for building an extension –

Figure 3.26 Perceived price reduction is affected by the distance between the numbers

Figure 3.27 The Weber–Fechner law: the higher the number, the smaller the perceived difference

it doesn't make much difference if it costs £50 more or less. However, if we're buying a pair of shoes at, say, £100, then £50 makes a big difference. To really make a perceived difference requires less of an absolute price increase or decrease in low-priced categories than in high-priced categories. So when we reduce prices we should think carefully about whether the proposed discount really is making a perceived difference. If not, we are only likely to reduce our revenue and hence our margin. The same logic, of course, applies if we want to maximize the potential of price increases. In addition, we must consider the effect of contrast. If new but similar price-based offers are constantly being made in a market, the consumer simply gets used to it. Under these conditions, the subjectively experienced contrast of the discount is reduced and it thereby loses its pain-relieving effect.

What we have learned in this chapter

- Perception is an active process in the brain which is based on past learning experiences.
- Peripheral perception is key for maximizing the effectiveness of our marketing.
- We have no picture memory. Recognition is determined by the most significant diagnostic cues and context.
- Signals we send – from colours to shapes to brand logos – are recoded into mental concepts based on learned associations in memory. Purchase decisions are mainly based on these mental concepts, and not on the signals as such.

What this means to us as marketers

- Our brands and products communicate with our consumers mainly through their blurred, peripheral vision. We need to use signals which effectively convey our messages even through this blurred vision.
- When refreshing or relaunching a brand it is not a question of how much we change, the key question is what we change. We need to be very careful when changing diagnostic cues. Given a mental concept we want to convey, we can be flexible in how we convey it, as long as the signals are intuitively linked to the desired mental concept. This allows more flexibility and freedom in execution but at the same time guarantees consistency on a conceptual level.
- The core driver of attention is the fit of peripheral signals with consumer goals. The higher the fit, the more we attract attention ('pull').

4

Optimizing the Path to Purchase

The Decision Interface Makes the Difference

We'll take the next step in our journey through the autopilot. The commonly held view in marketing is that, in order to change behaviour, it's first necessary to change attitudes. This chapter challenges that view and shows the profound influence that the 'decision interface' has on behaviour. We will identify key implicit decision rules and discover how to employ them to best effect in marketing.

Decision interfaces influence purchase decisions: a visit to the canteen

Imagine we are the principal of a college and are concerned about the health of our students. We want to improve their eating habits and reduce their calorie intake. What would be the best way to achieve this? We might come up with the idea of an internal 'advertising' campaign to inform the students about the benefits of healthy food, and to teach them more about the negatives of eating too many calories. Many studies in the area of health psychology suggest that such campaigns might indeed change attitudes towards high-calorie food, and also help to raise people's intention to eat more healthily, but these same studies also suggest that the resultant impact on actual behaviour is negligible.

We have all probably experienced this for ourselves. If we did act on our intentions then far fewer of us would smoke, and a BMI of above 25 would be rare. So, as principal, our next step might be to take more direct and severe actions in the student canteen, such as only serving healthy meals and cutting out everything that is unhealthy. But this probably would have limited effect since we can't stop the students going elsewhere to eat, for example to the unhealthy burger bar around the corner. So what other choices do we have?

Brian Wansink, John Dyson Professor of Consumer Behaviour at Cornell University and author of the best-seller *Mindless Eating: Why We Eat*

More Than We Think (2006), approached this topic in a very different way. In his experiment, he didn't change any items on the menu, he only changed the way in which the canteen was arranged and the way products were displayed. In other words, he did not change *what* was offered, he changed *how* it was presented – he changed the decision interface. Here are some examples of his rearrangements and the effects they had on food choice (see Figure 4.1):

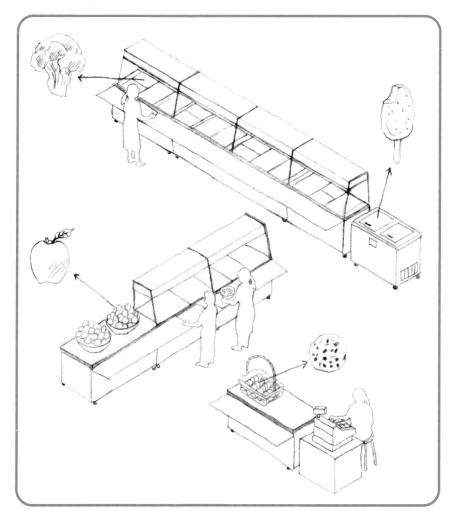

Figure 4.1 Illustration showing some of the changes in the Wansink canteen experiment

- Broccoli was moved to the very beginning of the lunch line, increasing its consumption by 10–15 per cent.
- Apples and oranges were put in a nice bowl instead of a stainless steel pan, more than doubling their sales.
- The lid of the ice-cream freezer was changed from transparent to opaque, reducing the proportion of students who chose ice cream from 30 per cent to 14 per cent.
- Including healthy desserts (fruit) within the price of the lunch, but having to pay separately for an unhealthy dessert like a cookie, led to 71 per cent more fruit being consumed and 55 per cent fewer cookies.
- Moving the chocolate milk behind the plain milk, making it difficult to reach without asking for help, led to more students choosing plain milk.
- Relocating the salad bar away from the wall and placing it in front of the checkout register nearly tripled sales of salads.

These changes in aggregate resulted in a significant decrease in calorie intake as well as a much healthier overall composition of the lunches consumed, despite the fact that the students were not aware that anything had changed. However, once the changes were reversed, the old eating behaviours came back.

How can such seemingly trivial changes in the decision interface – where something is placed, the visibility of items, the behavioural cost to obtain the item, etc. – have such a significant impact on purchase decisions? Why did the students buy more broccoli when the only difference to the usual arrangement was a change in the decision interface, i.e. placing it at the beginning of the lunch line? What are the underlying principles?

In the case of broccoli, the change meant that it was exposed at an early stage of the purchase choice process. Hence, the motivational context that the students are in when they enter the canteen is important. It's reasonable to assume that they're hungry and this acts as an internal trigger for the autopilot to search for options that fit their goal of physical satiation. The first item of food that they see in this context, therefore, is highly valued. Hence the perceived value of broccoli will be much higher when they have an empty plate than if their plate is already quite full with meat and French fries, as it would have been in the previous canteen arrangement. With a full plate the students would already have a mental sense of satiation, which would decrease the perceived value of any foodstuff coming later in their decision process. If we are hungry, we are more likely to fill our plate with the first item that solves that problem, leaving less space for the items to come.

Putting oranges in an attractive fruit bowl frames the fruit differently and hence increases its perceived value in the same way that packaging does. It just looks tastier and of higher value. The effect of the opaque lid on the ice-cream freezer impedes the first step in the decision-making process: perception. It prevents the signal of 'ice cream' being perceived and this, therefore, simply does not prompt the idea of having an ice cream (despite its high hedonic value). We've all probably experienced this when queuing at a checkout: the desire for a bar of chocolate while we wait is activated merely by seeing it. Without this signal our craving would not occur – out of sight is, quite literally, out of mind.

The same principle is at work in the example of the milk being rearranged. Placing the plain milk in front of the chocolate milk hinders the processing of the signal of chocolate. It also results in the need to ask someone serving in the canteen to pass it, which is an off-putting extra behavioural cost and especially so if other students are waiting behind you as this situation induces time pressure. The outcome of students choosing the plain milk was a result of it being easier to reach, i.e. it had a lower behavioural cost.

When it comes to buying cookies, the students have to pay the same price for the cookie whether they buy it separately or as part of a 'meal deal'.

However, from the point of view of perception, these two ways of paying are very different. In the meal deal, the specific price of the cookie is not perceived at the moment of purchase. Students know that it costs something, but there is no perceivable signal to indicate precisely what this is. So the perceived cost is low. Having to pay separately for the cookie makes the price salient and this makes the pain tangible, thus increasing the perceived cost. The result is that the balance of the value–cost equation is adjusted such that purchase of the cookie is less likely.

In early 2012 Google adopted a similar approach for their canteens. Let's look at some examples of what they did:

- Sweets are no longer in clear hanging dispensers, instead you have to reach into less obvious opaque bins, resulting in a 9 per cent drop of caloric intake from sweets in just one week.
- Since people tend to fill their plates with whatever they see first, the first thing you experience on entering the canteen is the salad bar.
- Options are coloured – green labels are paired with vegetables; most desserts have red labels – using clear signals to make it tangible which options are or are not healthy.
- In the past, water was on tap and soda was in the fridge. Now bottled water is at eye level in the cooler, while soda has been moved to the bottom. That shift in placement increased water intake by 47 per cent.

The similarities to the Wansink lunch line study are obvious and the impact of the changes is just as striking. The principle that behaviour is highly influenced by the decision interface even works for nutrition experts, as another study by Brian Wansink shows. The experts were attending an 'ice-cream social' to celebrate the success of a colleague. They were randomly given either a small or a large bowl and either a small or a large ice-cream scoop. Even though they were experts on nutrition, when they were given a larger bowl they served themselves 31 per cent more ice cream without being aware of it. Their servings increased by 14 per cent when they were given a larger serving scoop.

What these examples show is not exclusive to food consumption. They illustrate a general, fundamental result of decision science: that decisions are strongly influenced not only by *what* is presented but, to a high degree, by *how* it is presented. Classical economic theory is unable to explain these effects because the objective value and the objective costs of the lunch items have not changed. Broccoli is broccoli, whether it is placed at the beginning or in the middle of the lunch line.

Value perception and decision making are influenced not only by **what** *is presented but also by* **how** *it is presented.*

Interfaces change behaviour without changing minds

Changing minds in order to change behaviour is at the core of what we as marketers have always done. We have been led to believe that non-users have a lack of knowledge about our products, and so we try to convince them to buy by telling them what we think is important. We attempt to induce a positive attitude by producing entertaining TV ads, hoping that the positive affect (in the psychological sense of the feeling they experience) from watching the ad will positively influence their attitudes towards the brand. Pre-testing methods that are typically used present strong evidence of the belief that behaviour is driven by attitudes only: we measure mostly respondents' stated intentions and attitudes. We evaluate what contributions the product, packaging or advertisement make to the brand image, and the effectiveness of the test stimulus is concluded from whether consumers show positive attitudes towards it or not. The focus is consistently on the person, and not on the context in which that person decides. The assumption is that we need to provide non-customers with persuasive arguments and information in order to change their attitudes about our product and brand which will result in congruently adjusted purchase behaviour.

This is certainly not wrong, and we will take a look at the person side of the equation in the next chapter, but it is far from complete. We have already witnessed the fact that any behaviour is an interaction between situational, external and personal, intrinsic factors. The lunch line example shows that there is a decision-making process that is not based on attitudes and intentions but, rather, on the concrete, perceptible experience at the precise moment and situational context in which a decision is made. The fact that peripheral, yet tangible, signals and subtle behavioural consequences influence purchase decisions raises another, even more fundamental point: decisions are not only driven by attitudes. So, behaviour change does not have to be preceded by a change in attitudes. People's choices can be influenced by changing the 'decision interface' and thus the context which defines the perceivable characteristics of the moment of decision making.

That we can change behaviour without changing minds is one of the core insights of behavioural economics. This insight is so profound that both the UK and the US governments have now set up units to exploit this knowledge in areas of public policy. They are using it to better understand and influence citizens' decisions in energy usage, health care, crime and road safety. Using the type of road signs that flash up the approaching motorist's speed, local authorities added another signal to that of the speed itself: a smiley face device. So whenever someone drove towards the sign within the speed limit, they would see a smiling face (see Figure 4.2), but if they drove too fast, the sad face with the mouth turned down appeared. These signals increased the number of drivers following the rules and significantly decreased accidents as a result. The sign was even more effective than standard speed cameras, at a fraction of the cost.

The smiley works because it provides meaning to the speed displayed, since a number without reference is hard for the autopilot to understand.

Figure 4.2 Signals trigger behavioural change. SID – Speed Indication Display Image supplied with permission of Traffic Technology Ltd

It also works better than the traditional solutions because immediate feedback triggers behavioural change more strongly than receiving a fine weeks or months later. The frowning face directly addresses our autopilot, notifying our excessive speed at the point where the decision needs to be addressed. In contrast to any subsequent fine, the frowning face signal is tangible at the very moment when the decision is made.

The proximity to the point of decision is a key factor for signals to influence behaviour. Taking a familiar marketing example, promotional mechanics qualify themselves perfectly for such effects since the interface occurs directly when the decision takes place. In a study, scientists looked at the impact of different promotions on sales of Snickers bars. The first promotion consisted only of a call to action ('buy some for your freezer'). This promotion resulted in average sales of

The interface influences decision making and purchases without prior change in consumer attitudes. This provides us, as marketers, with an additional approach for influencing consumer behaviour, beyond the prevailing model of having to change attitudes first.

1.4 bars. Then they changed the promotion by adding a behavioural anchor: 'Buy 18 for your freezer.' This might appear ridiculous, but the impact was significant. The average number of bars sold this time was 2.6. In neither case was the price discounted. Simply by adding the higher number as a perceivable and tangible anchor they almost doubled the sales – without a preceding step of changing attitudes.

One area where these insights are particularly useful is that of interactive media. It's almost impossible to write a brand strategy these days without including social media, interactive media and web 2.0. In many strategy documents the interactive world is an extension of the 360-degree implementation of a campaign; a Facebook page and a YouTube channel are produced alongside a new TV ad. Viewed through the lens of behavioural economics, we can now differentiate the roles of touchpoints more precisely in order to exploit their full potential.

Imagine waiting for the train to show up and looking at a poster. How could we turn this passive touchpoint into an interactive one? Tesco in Korea and Peapod in Chicago use interactive billboards like a virtual shelf where consumers are able to place their order using their smartphones while waiting for the train so that they can subsequently pick up the order at the store.

The ubiquity of interactive media now offers marketers more decision interfaces than ever before, thereby creating opportunities to be close to the moment of truth. This ability to be 'in the moment' qualifies interactive media to create perceived value and/or reduce perceived cost in the purchase decision process, or even to create new decision interfaces altogether. The Solarchecker app from SMA which we encountered earlier is an example of a new touchpoint at a stage within the decision-making process to which the brand did not previously have access. Another example of this is provided by Westpac Bank. Inspired by a TED (Technology, Entertainment, Design) talk by Rory Sutherland, they wanted to

Figure 4.3 Simply press to save

encourage their customers to save more money, and their idea was to enable people to show the same impulsive behaviour when saving as they do when buying things. People always have good intentions to save but simply do not do so because the behavioural cost is prohibitive – it seems too much effort to go to the bank, phone or even carry out a transaction online. So Westpac created a mobile app, called Impulse Saver, through which customers can transfer a set amount of money from their current account to their savings account simply by pressing a big red virtual button on their phone (see Figure 4.3).

This is more than just another mobile touchpoint – it creates a new decision interface. It enables consumers to behave in line with their intentions directly and 'in the moment' by reducing the behavioural costs. No need to go to a branch or to call them or to wait until you have access to online banking. Additionally, the amounts you can save can be very small, with the consequence that the 'pain' that the customer experiences with each transaction is lower. No one would bother to drive to the bank and then fill out a form merely to transfer £2 from one account

Recent developments in interactive media provide powerful interfaces which are there in the moment when decisions are made. This allows us to create new and innovative decision interfaces with customers.

to another, or spend 10 minutes online doing the same. So the interface works by being there in the moment we want to save, thereby enabling us to save on impulse.

The cases so far have shown that behaviour can be influenced without changing the attitudes of consumers. But there is another interesting twist to this new opportunity area. Not only are decisions driven by the interface, but the resulting actions can, in turn, change attitudes. Dan Ariely refers to this as 'self-herding': when we believe something is good (or bad) on the basis of our own previous behaviour. In his 2010 book *Predictably Irrational*, Ariely provides the following example:

> *Imagine that something happens that makes you feel happy and generous – say, your favorite team wins the World Series. That night you are having dinner at your mother-in-law's and, while in this great mood, impulsively decide to buy her flowers. A month later, the emotion of the big win has faded away and so has the cash in your wallet. It is time for another visit to your mother-in-law. You think about how a good son-in-law should act. You consult your memory, and you remember your wonderful flower-buying act from your last visit, so you repeat it. You then repeat the ritual over and over until it becomes a habit (and in general this is not a bad habit to fall into). Even though the underlying reason for your initial action (excitement over the game) is no longer present, you take your past actions as an indication of what you should do next and the kind of son-in-law you are (the kind who buys his mother-in-law flowers). That way, the effects of the initial emotion end up influencing a long string of decisions.*

Self-herding is when, rather than copying what a bunch of other people in a public place are doing, we refer to our own actions in the past for implicit guidance. Peripheral situational factors influence our decisions – such as the example we saw earlier, when the students' increased consumption of broccoli was encouraged by its earlier presence in the canteen layout. This decision will, in turn, shape their attitudes towards broccoli. The next time they choose it they will value it more highly simply because they chose it last time. By creating a new, easier decision interface there is a higher frequency of interaction with the brand or product which leads to an improvement in attitude towards it because the more often we use something, the higher we value it. For service brands especially, where the value delivered is mostly intangible and the frequency of interaction is low, these marketing tools provide a huge opportunity.

We can recognize this effect in brand image research as well: consumers show more positive attitudes towards strong brands that they have used at least a few times in their lives. The adjusted attitudes are an outcome of purchase decisions. Actions do not merely reveal preferences but rather create them. Following this perspective of 'attitudes follow actions', actions can, and do, create preferences and biased memories, and then reinforce them. So, once students start eating broccoli because it is visible early on in the lunch line, their attitude towards broccoli will eventually change for the better. The corollary for marketing is that generating trial is crucial to change attitudes. Increasing penetration is a means to influence the attitude towards a brand.

Increasing trial (i.e. penetration) is a means to influence the attitude towards a brand because behaviour results in attitude change. Again, this offers a new and powerful alternative to traditional thinking that behaviour change requires a prior change in attitudes.

Decision interfaces are very powerful, yet they often don't get the attention they deserve. We normally do not think of specific interfaces and contexts to be purchase drivers, so they receive little management consideration. Applying the implicit perspective of perceived value and cost along every step in the purchasing process can reveal new possibilities for increasing sales. These can be a significant source of business if they are optimized with insights from psychology in general, and from behavioural economics in particular. This approach to behaviour change is complementary to one focusing on the person and his or her goals or attitudes. Its major benefit is to optimize the path to purchase: to increase perceived value and/or lower perceived barriers. So let's have a look at the marketing interfaces which can profit from behavioural economics. In so doing we will consider those instances where the consumer interacts directly, or needs to respond or make a decision at a particular moment.

Incremental innovations with huge impact

In marketing, we are constantly searching for possibilities to gain a competitive edge over the competition by developing new products and new product features and improving product quality. And of course this is necessary. However, what we just saw illustrates that there is a big opportunity to gain competitive edge by improving the decision interface through changing small things at low cost. The impact can be highly disproportionate to the investment required. In the report by the UK Institute for Government and the Cabinet office on their behavioural economics approach to policy making, the authors write:

> *Approaches based on 'changing contexts' – the environment within which we make decisions and respond to cues – have the potential to bring about significant changes in behaviour at relatively low cost. Shaping policy more closely around our in-built responses to the world offers a potentially powerful way to improve individual well-being and social welfare.*

It does not require much imagination to see that the same conclusion holds for marketing: if we shape our marketing even more closely around in-built consumer responses to the world, we will be even more successful and have an additional lever for sales. So, let's look more concretely at how this can help. Scientists conducted a field experiment with a carwash and its customers using 'loyalty cards' as the decision interface. Customers

Figure 4.4 The pre-stamped card triggered twice the number of sales

had the card stamped each time they used the carwash and they could collect stamps to obtain a free wash. One half of the customer base required ten stamps in order to receive the free wash. As a little gift, the cards had already been stamped twice – therefore, another eight car washes were required for a free wash. The other half of the customers received a very similar card, except there were no 'free' stamps to start with and there were only eight stamps in total rather than ten (see Figure 4.4). So, objectively, both groups of customers had to buy eight car washes in order to get the free one.

One would assume that both cards would lead to the same result, as both groups had an identical reward on offer and both had to pay for eight washes in order to achieve it. But something entirely different happened in reality. The scientists found that those customers who had received the pre-stamped cards were *twice* as likely to buy the additional eight car-washes at this specific facility compared with the group without the free stamps. What happened here? The signal of 'two stamps' had triggered what's known as 'process endowment': the card holder was already on his way to filling the card and this activated the goal to finish the process. Framing the task as one that has already been started and is incomplete rather than one that has not yet begun leads to people being more committed to completing the task and, moreover, they complete the task more quickly. This small and cost-neutral change to the decision interface had a significant impact on sales. Process endowment is also one reason why we are more likely to wait for the completion of a download or installation when a progress bar is displayed. We are already on our way, so we want to finish it.

The following example shows that seemingly trivial changes to the decision interface can have a positive impact on revenue and sales. Consider the effect of a small but perceptible change to the menu in a restaurant offering a daily 'special'. Researchers at Cornell University investigated how the way pricing is displayed influences the turnover of a restaurant. The prices on a menu were displayed in three different ways (see Figure 4.5):

Numerical with Euro sign:	10,00 €
Numerical without Euro sign:	10
In written form:	Ten euro

In terms of the highest sales, the scientists expected the 'ten euro' version to be the most successful, as using words rather than numbers makes it harder to do the maths and hence control how much has already been ordered. But this was not the case. The numerical display without the Euro sign was the most successful. Each table spent a full €5 more if they had menus with prices not referencing the Euro, compared with the two other groups. Prices activate the pain area in the brain, and this result shows that the pain was perceived to be higher when the € signal or 'Euro' wording was tangible. Without a tangible and hence perceivable signal for cost, the price was perceived to be less costly. This tiny change, one which was easy and cost nothing to implement, had a huge impact on the customers' purchase decisions and resulted in increased revenue for the restaurant.

Small changes in decision interfaces can have a disproportionate impact on perceived net value and thus sales.

Figure 4.5 The way the price is presented has significant impact on revenue

The starting point for inspiring innovation and ideas is to look at which touchpoints we have with the consumer. Let's take the example of an energy supplier. Like many other service companies the touchpoints are quite rare. Normally we do not contact our energy supplier if everything is working well. The most regular contact point is likely to be the bill. The US company Opower shows how this touchpoint, which normally has negative associations of cost, can be used to add value and to change the behaviour of customers. They printed bar charts on the bills showing an individual customer's energy usage in comparison with the average of other people in the same street, together with simple messages either praising the customer for using less than his neighbours or suggesting energy-efficient ways that the customer could reduce his future usage to match that of his neighbours (see Figure 4.6).

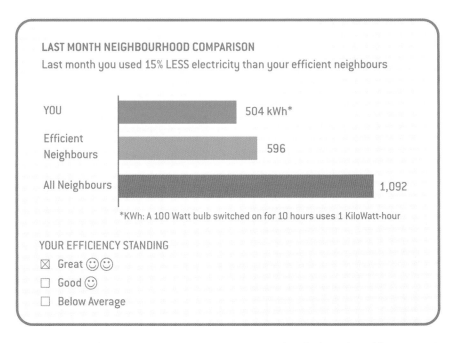

Figure 4.6 Displaying energy consumption compared with that of neighbours signifi-cantly impacts future behaviour

This simple and inexpensive measure had the same effect on reducing energy consumption as a price increase of 20 per cent. This change in behaviour does not diminish over time either, as long-term studies show. Again, the approach here is not to convince people through campaigns and information. Instead, what is used in this case is the realization that people often follow social norms. We tend to do what those around us are already doing. We all know this influence of social proof from everyday life. Which bar are you more likely to enter: one with only two customers present or one with 20? Which rating on Amazon do you trust more: one based on two responses or one from 200 people? Lots of scientific research shows that communicating what others do in similar situations is a powerful way to change behaviour. When a hotel room contained a sign that asked guests to recycle their towels to help save the environment, 35 per cent did so. When the sign also said that most guests at the hotel recycled their towels at least once during their stay, 44 per cent complied. And when the sign said that most previous occupants *of that particular room* had reused towels at some point during their stay, 49 per cent of guests in that room then recycled. The power of social norms increases if we relate them to the target audience as closely as possible, such as when comparing energy consumption against that of neighbours. In the case of Opower, this 'social proof' activated the comparison with relevant others: their neighbours. As every value is relative, this comparison leads to a re-evaluation of one's own behaviour and, hence, to behavioural change.

One principle that shows up in most of the examples we have looked at so far is that we dislike losses more than we like gains of an equivalent amount, i.e. we are loss averse. Loss aversion is a fundamental facet of human decision making. So let's have a closer look at its relevance for marketing. In order to encourage people to buy a product we often communicate a call to action, in which it is common to focus on telling consumers how much they can save. As this reduces the perceived pain, it works. However, the 'how' of the saving makes a difference. An energy company in the US found that when they communicated to their customers that switching to energy-saving mode would save (and therefore they would gain) $200 a year, it had very low take-up. However, when they changed the message to show that by not switching to energy-saving mode they would lose $200, there was an extremely positive response. The mechanism behind that is loss aversion: avoiding loss is valued more highly than gaining something of the same monetary value. When deciding whether to accept a gamble that offers a 50/50 chance of winning or losing money, people typically accept only those bets in which the amount that could be gained is at least twice the amount that could be lost (e.g. a 50/50 chance either to gain $100 or to lose $50). Most measures of loss aversion find that people place approximately twice the value on giving up an item than they do on receiving it. Like the saying 'a bird in the hand is worth two in the bush', the value–cost equation in the autopilot is skewed, indicating that emphasizing the money that people will lose by not taking an action will motivate them more than telling them what they can save.

Loss aversion is one major barrier for people when it comes to switching brands or adopting innovations: the risk of losing some-thing we value can be exceeded only by offering twice the value. We sometimes come across this in focus groups. Consumers talk positively about a new product or service, but when asked whether they want to exchange the product they currently use for the new one, they suddenly start to reject the new one in favour of what they have. Very often the point is not to get across the best possible value but to avoid the threat of incurring a loss or being disappointed.

Interfaces, even simple ones like an energy bill or a collector card with two stamps, trigger implicit decision rules which then result in a behaviour change.

Principles of persuasive decision interfaces

Small changes in the decision interface can have a huge impact on purchase decisions and sales. The underlying mechanisms in these examples like process endowment, social proof or loss aversion are automated decision rules – heuristics – that can be deliberately activated by the interface and that, in turn, influence our perception of value and cost. These heuristics are rules of thumb that the brain uses in response to situations and environments. They are fully automatic and thus allow for rapid, autopilot decision making with little effort. The benefit of these decision rules is that we can decide very quickly and intuitively without energy-consuming reflective thinking.

The systematic use of heuristics allows us to manage each decision inter-face along the path to purchase in order to influence choice and thus help to create sales growth opportunities. The dominant decision interface with the customer in packaged consumer goods is the point of sale (POS) in the supermarket. Depending on the category, 40–70 per cent of all purchase decisions are made at the POS with little pre-planning, indicating that the decision is largely influenced by the signals present. So even at the POS where consumers are usually assumed to be clear about what they want to buy, concrete signals make the difference. This is what Rory Sutherland refers to in the following quotation:

> *In making decisions, conscious or unconscious, big or small, about our lives and what we buy and do, the context, framework, decision interface, medium and pathways through which we reach decisions may have a greater influence on the decisions we take than the long-term consequences of the decision.*

A challenge remains, however. There are literally dozens of implicit decision rules that science has uncovered. This can be overwhelming for practitioners at times. So in order to make this interesting and valuable field more manageable, let's have a look at the overriding principles that help to systematically increase the persuasiveness of the decision interfaces we have with our customers.

The following three meta-principles help to understand why customers do not exhibit the behaviour that we would like them to, and to optimize our decision interfaces accordingly:

1. *Tangibility*: to trigger heuristics, there must be tangible and perceptible signals.
2. *Immediacy*: the autopilot prefers immediate rewards compared with future rewards.
3. *Certainty*: the autopilot prefers the safe, certain choice.

As we will see in the remainder of this chapter, understanding these principles is enormously helpful in optimizing the path to purchase and the respective decision interfaces.

Tangibility – no signal no action

To illustrate what tangibility is about let's have a look at a technology with significant potential for marketing: augmented reality. Lego devised an augmented reality system allowing a Lego box to be held up to a screen in store and the finished product to then be displayed sitting on top of the box (see Figure 4.7). The idea is to show parents and their children what the finished Lego construction, the one they were considering buying, would look like before purchase. Research has shown that the longer somebody touches a product, the more likely they are to purchase that

Figure 4.7 Virtual reality makes the product more tangible and increases perceived value. Sourced from 'Augmented Reality Lego Display' http://legoeducationalresource. blogspot.co.uk. Reproduced with permission of LEGO UK

product, so holding the product up to access this display is a benefit in itself. By showing them a virtual product, this can drive and uplift sales because the benefit, the value of the product, becomes more tangible.

Swiss watchmaker Tissot has also made use of this principle by enabling window shoppers to try on its luxury watches from the sidewalk. Shop windows are transformed into an interactive shopping experience where, by using a camera and touchscreen system, 3D technology turns a paper wristband into any Tissot watch. Consumers not only see how the watches look on their wrists, they can also experiment with the corresponding touchscreen features, for example the compass, altimeter and thermometer, of those watches. In addition, those trying out watches can take a picture of themselves and post it to Twitter or Instagram for a chance to win the watch of their choice every week of the campaign. The Tissot campaign was more successful than any of its previous campaigns in Britain. Sales in the Tissot Selfridges boutique rose 83 per cent.

The luxury French jeweller Boucheron allowed consumers to 'virtually' try on their jewellery pieces from home or via smartphone, causing a 50 per cent increase in website traffic.

Augmented reality is also interesting and potentially valuable for all retailers. Angela Maurer, head of innovation at Tesco, says: 'With Tesco it allows customers to try before they buy. It is an important element to use because it reassures customers and they can visualize items they want to purchase.' However, she warns that it is vital for retailers to make the experience simple for customers. In other words, the experience must be compatible for our autopilot – only then will it add real value. We should not use technology just because it's trendy, we should do it to add value to the consumer experience, especially since it implies additional behavioural costs (e.g. downloading an app, investing time to use it).

In order to influence the perceived net value of something, we need tangible signals. Without a signal, heuristics cannot be triggered.

Tangible signals at the POS can influence the way people shop. Imagine an oral care aisle. Normally people know what they need: toothpaste or a toothbrush. However, research shows that if the store aisle sends signals that activate a broader concept such as 'dental health', then consumers purchase not only the intended item but additional complementary items as well. If consumers approach the fixture in a very concrete mindset ('I want toothpaste'), they tend to buy only this item. When they have a more general, broader mindset ('I want to improve the health of my teeth'), they are more likely to purchase complementary items as well. This broader mindset can be induced by tangible signals in the environment, for example by placing signals relating to 'healthy teeth' at the beginning of the oral care aisle, or framing a multi-product promotion using this broader mindset.

Tangibility, as a principle, is helpful in order for us to better understand perceived cost. We need to prevent sending signals that increase the perceived costs, as illustrated by the earlier example showing the impact of removing the € symbol from the menu. Another case in point is the 'Keep the Change' programme run by the Bank of America. With this free service, all purchases are rounded up to the next even amount and the difference is added to a savings account. By doing this, the saving could not only be made with no additional behavioural cost, it also made the pain of saving less tangible. As with the example of the cookies in the lunch line, it makes a difference if the amount of money we spend (or save) is tangible or not. Since its launch in 2005, 'Keep the Change' has led to more than 12 million new customers and more than $3.1 billion in savings for them.

The tangibility of costs is worth considering when thinking about tariff structures. Imagine you have to decide on the payment mechanism for membership of a gym. Upon first consideration we are unlikely to assume that the way people pay for their membership could have an impact on our business. Even if we assumed that it would, we would probably think that payment of an annual membership fee upfront would make the pain intangible for the rest of the year. This would lead us to think that this mechanism might be better. So, which type of payment scheme is likely to result in more people visiting the gym: the one asking for an upfront payment of the yearly fee of £600 or the one asking for a monthly payment of £50? Research shows that those who pay monthly are reminded more often that the gym costs money – it makes the costs more tangible – and this makes them visit the gym more frequently. After each payment, the number of visits shoots up, only to slowly return to a baseline level. Making the cost more tangible in this case has a beneficial effect: more visits imply more fitness and thus greater perceived value. Loyalty increases through the more frequent visits triggered by the monthly fee.

This effect is based on the 'sunk cost' heuristic that goes along with the tangibility of the cost: we want to avoid having paid something for nothing. If we have paid for it then we want to use it. Thus it can be advantageous to expose costs, rather than hide them, in some instances. This depends on which behaviour we want the decision interface to trigger, i.e. which behaviour best meets our marketing objectives.

To make use of the tangibility principle to improve decision interfaces, the following questions can help. Which signals are tangible along the purchase decision process? Which signals make reward and pain tangible? Which signals should be changed in order to improve the perceived value–cost relationship?

Immediacy – I want it NOW!

Another key principle for persuasive decision interfaces is immediacy. The autopilot is strongly biased by the present, by what it perceives in the moment. Hence future consequences that are not yet perceivable have much less impact on our decisions. Value and costs are discounted by distance. For example, seeing a tiger far away triggers different responses compared with when it is close to us. In an experiment in 2010, neuro-economist

Antonio Rangel from Caltech showed that people paid up to 60 per cent more for an item of fast food if the item was actually physically present compared with a visual or textual presentation. The study also found that if the item was presented behind Plexiglas, rather than being available for someone to simply grab, the willingness to pay was reduced. The shorter the distance, the higher the perceived value and the lower the perceived barriers to obtain it.

This holds true for distance in time as well. Getting ill in 20 years is not as threatening as having a headache tomorrow. We usually prefer smaller, more immediate payoffs to larger, more distant ones. The offer of £100 today may be preferred to the promise of one of £120 next year. Behavioural economists refer to this as 'hyperbolic discounting': we have a very high discount rate for the future compared with the here and now. This is why we discount the future very heavily when sacrifices are required in the present, such as stopping smoking or exercising more often. We recognize this from our own experience: we all know that we should adopt a healthier lifestyle in order to prevent illness in the future, but this consequence is not currently perceivable to us and this allows us to opt for the cigarette and the beer because their value is available to us right now. This future discounting is the reason why we tend to spend more when using credit cards – the pain of paying is deferred to some future moment.

In terms of our perception, the more immediate the reward, the better, and the later the cost, the better.

How can we make use of this in marketing? The automotive category is a good example where car manufacturers regularly create special offers – most of them are discount mechanisms. Fiat, for example, in 2012 addressed the future discounting of the autopilot very overtly. Their offer is that customers pay half of the purchase price now and then pay the second half in two years' time. In their TV ads they highlight the first payment (€5,900), thereby making the tangible cost low. The second cost is mentally discounted by the customer due to the time distance in the future.

A similar innovation called the 'gym pact' was created by behavioural economists at Harvard. They were addressing a well-known barrier: going to the gym regularly. Here, again, the benefit is future based, but we face behavioural and monetary costs in the present. The 'gym pact' changes the game. Members commit to a certain number of workouts per week. If they meet this commitment they have to pay a certain amount, but can also earn money back if they stick to their commitments, and they pay more if they miss them. So, if members don't behave as they intended then they increase their own costs today and, in so doing, also make the negative consequences, that were previously associated with the future, tangible today. Applying the basic principle of adding value and reducing cost by applying the 'immediacy' principle in this way to the membership mechanic works brilliantly.

If you think of promotions such as free prize draws, applying this principle can explain differences in responses. If the potential prize is postponed to a moment in the future, the value is discounted by this distance. And this perspective is useful when thinking about innovative promotional mechanics.

One successful example of leveraging this potential is the German smartphone app known as 'Wynshen' (the pronunciation of this word is identical to the German word for 'wishing'). This is a point-of-sale app for both shoppers and retailers in shopping malls. Shoppers take a photo of a product in which they're interested, in a participating store, and send it to Wynshen. A random generator on the app then immediately shows what the shopper has 'won'. This may be a discount on that particular product or a related one – or even a voucher for a free coffee in the nearby Starbucks. There are also lotteries with larger prizes. This app reduces the response latency of a prize

To utilize the immediacy principle to improve decision interfaces, the following questions can help. How great is the distance in time and space to the tangible perception of value and cost? And how can this distance be reduced (in the case of making value more immediate) or increased (for putting cost further into the future)?

draw to almost zero – the reward is obtained in the moment rather than at some point in the distant future. Hence the app increases perceived value for a very small behavioural cost, and it has been successful in increasing both sales and dwell time in stores. Overall these examples show that perceived value and cost can be significantly influenced by the actual time at which the value and cost are, literally, perceived.

Certainty – the bird in the hand

The third principle after tangibility and immediacy is certainty. Overall, certainty is about the expected probability of, and the perceived risk in, obtaining reward and incurring pain. Certainty is the perceived chance of obtaining the value and/or preventing the cost. This is the reason why promotions with a higher chance of winning are more effective – knowing that one in a hundred customers wins something is less powerful than a win ratio of one in ten.

Let's have a look at some examples that illustrate the certainty principle. Imagine shopping in a foreign country where we are not familiar with any of the brands. Which one would we pick? We might go for the one with the most shelf space, as this indicates that this brand is used by many other customers and hence will probably do the job. This significantly reduces the perceived risk of the purchase decision and thus increases the certainty of obtaining the value. Another example of the certainty princi-ple is that we value things we already own particularly highly. Nothing is more certain than holding something in our hands. Consumers who were given a coffee mug demanded twice as much to give it up as other con-sumers were willing to pay for it. Behavioural economists refer to this bias as the 'endowment effect'.

Something that's still with us from thousands of years ago is the so-called 'scarcity value'. We value things that appear to be a scarce resource because we don't know when they will be available again and therefore we want to ensure that we get them. While scarcity was a fact of life for our ancestors but is hardly something that affects our lives today, this heuristic is still active. Therefore signals of scarcity increase the perceived value of an object. In a study this heuristic was used, this time with a Campbells canned soup promotion. The first variant of the promotion was a straightforward '12 per cent off' price reduction. This resulted in an average purchase of 3.3 cans. The second variant added a scarcity signal: '12 per cent off. Maximum 4 cans per person.' This signalled that quantities were limited and caused a slight increase in sales to an average of 3.5 cans. However, the third promotional variant was: '12 per cent off. Maximum 12 cans per person.' This had a dramatic effect on average sales – they rose to 7 cans! It is likely that 12 acted as an anchor, but, in addition, the scarcity heuristic made people try to exploit the promotion. The signal made Campbells soups appear scarce, thereby increasing the value of the item and the value of having it.

So, if an item is in short supply and/or we don't know when it will be available again, our instinct is to hoard (as we did thousands of years ago with foodstuffs over the winter months). In the spring of 2012, the UK government advised car drivers to 'top up their tanks' due to the impending threat of a fuel tanker drivers' strike. Petrol stations were immediately besieged with queues of drivers and quickly ran out of fuel. It's perhaps ironic that a government that promotes behavioural economics didn't realize that the signal it sent triggered the scarcity effect, and that this became a self-fulfilling prophecy once drivers saw others queuing for petrol.

Another case that is based on the certainty principle is the flat rate bias. Whether it is telecommunications, internet or eating out, we have a preference for flat rates. People often prefer flat rates even though they are not necessarily the optimal choice. For example, from a monetary point of view, more than half the customers on flat rates in the telecoms market would actually be better off with a usage-based tariff. So why do they prefer flat rates? Consumers do not know how much the future cost will be, so there is a risk in having a higher, unpredictable cost. Research shows that if the telco invoice exceeds the amount that a customer expects, then the difference between expected and real costs is highly magnified. This gap results in a much higher perceived cost, so it motivates consumers to prevent this situation from happening. Therefore they opt for a flat-rate tariff so they can be sure about the costs.

The more certain the perceived reward, the better, and the more certain the loss prevention, the better.

The heuristic to follow what others do – social proof – is largely based on this principle as well. We follow the behaviour of others to avoid risk and to maximize the certainty of getting value for our money, be it on Amazon when buying a book or on a travel site when evaluating a hotel for our next holiday. The fact that we value the safe choice also shows in our preference for defaults. Most people never change the default settings in their browsers or mobile phones. We very often go with whatever the default is because in most cases, and most of the time, the default works just fine, it is the safe choice. Moreover it allows the brain to operate on autopilot mode, the cognitive 'ease' consumes less energy.

How far this default heuristic can impact our decisions is illustrated by the following example. Every year thousands of people die because a donor organ cannot be found for them in time. Politicians and medical bodies in many countries campaign to improve donor rates. Have a look at the graph in Figure 4.8 which shows donor consent rates in different countries. Some have very high rates (e.g. Austria and France) while others have very low ones (e.g. the UK, Germany).

The difference between the countries is not their degree of morality or their social or religious orientation – it is simply down to how the forms are designed and therefore what the autopilot receives as input. In the UK you have to actively register as a donor ('opt-in'). In Austria, people are donors by default, unless they decide against it ('opt-out') (see Figure 4.9).

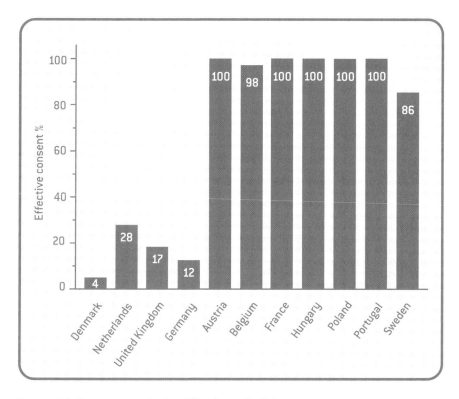

Figure 4.8 Donor consent rates differ dramatically by country

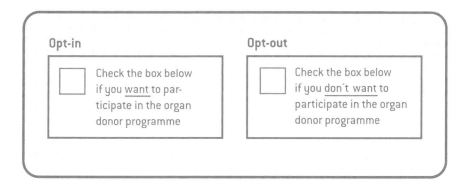

Figure 4.9 Opting in versus opting out of organ donation makes a huge difference

The default is the only difference and it has a significant impact on decision making. In the Netherlands, the Department of Health not only sent out letters to every citizen, they also ran a door-to-door campaign begging people to donate. This resulted in a 28 per cent consent rate. Clearly, a simple and inexpensive change in the form to set the default to opt-out is much more effective.

Other studies have shown that consumers who are obliged to 'opt out' of an emailing list are twice as likely to stay on the list as consumers who can explicitly choose between receiving and not receiving the emails. We automatically associate ticking a box with agreement with something – no matter if this is objectively true or not. Moreover, based on experience we assume that the default is the safe choice.

To make use of the certainty principle to improve decision interfaces, the following questions need to be answered. How big is the perceived certainty of value and cost? And how can the perceived value be increased and the perceived cost be reduced?

Clever design of defaults can have a real impact on sales. In 2007, New York City forced cab drivers to begin taking credit cards, which involved installing a touch-screen system for payment. During payment, the user is presented with three buttons or defaults for tipping: 20 per cent, 25 per cent and 30 per cent (see Figure 4.10). When cabs were cash only, the average tip was roughly 10 per cent. After the introduction of this system, the tip percentage jumped to 22 per cent. The three buttons resulted in $144 million of additional tips per year!

How it all works together

How can we use the learnings from behavioural economics to optimize the decision interfaces we have with our customers? Figure 4.11 provides a summary of the principles we have looked at so far.

Figure 4.10 Defaults changed tipping behaviour in New York City cabs
Source: http://goodexperience.com/2011/02/how-a-taxi-button-cha.php

Decision Drivers / BE Principles	Value	Cost
Tangibility What is perceivable? (now or later)	Signals that make value tangible (vs. claimed)	Reduce cost signals Reframe
Immediacy When are value/cost delivered?	Future discounting Now > Future Minimize delay to reward Simplify process to reward	Future > Now Maximize delay to cost
Certainty What is the certainty of value/cost?	Maximize certainty of reward Endowment, social proof, scarcity	Minimize perceived probability/risk of incurring loss Defaults, satisficing, non-loss

Figure 4.11 Summary of meta-principles from behavioural economics

151

The following example shows that, within one interface, several principles and heuristics can be used to optimize the path to purchase. Groupon.com is a website that spurred a lot of interest when Google offered $6 billion to buy it (which they refused). The problems the company has faced more recently may have many reasons, but the design of the website is not one of them (see Figure 4.12). If your goal is to sell coupons online, this website does a pretty good job. Let's apply the principles in order to better understand why.

The first principle is the tangibility of value. Consumers see what they get. Value is very prominent because people are about to buy food in a restaurant. This is not only mentioned in the copy but portrayed visually. The value is also signalled next to the normal price, literally, by reframing the regular

Figure 4.12 The Groupon.com decision interface integrates several heuristics

152

price as 'value' rather than 'regular price'. The words 'limited quantity available' trigger the scarcity heuristic and this, together with the time limitation, also increases the perceived value. What about the cost side? Next to reducing the objective cost, the amount saved is shown prominently and in two formats: discount in per cent and savings in dollars. The regular price serves as an anchor through which the amount saved appears high. Immediacy is implemented by the highly salient 'Buy!' button – the reward can be hunted down with the click of one hot button. Through the time limit a sense of urgency is induced, which makes the hot button even more salient. Referring to the number of people who already purchased this item signals social proof which decreases both the uncertainty and the perceived risk of buying from what might be an unknown vendor. This reduces the perceived costs and works against loss aversion. In addition, scarcity is a call to action because certainty of value can be maximized only by acting now.

Another area where behavioural economics principles have been used successfully is saving for pensions. Everyone knows that we need to save money now in order to be better off in the future. So why does knowing this not result in us doing it? In order to address this, let's apply some of the principles we've seen so far. Since it is all about perceptible signals, we have to look at what value and what cost are perceivable when we save for our pension. The only tangible signal is the amount (cost) we have to save month by month. At the precise moment that we have to decide how much we are going to save we experience pain because we're giving money away. In order to accept this, we need to see a value in doing so. Yet at this same moment the value side is not perceptible – we know it's good to save, and the right thing to do, but we don't experience any value. The value is far away in the future and this discounts the value to the autopilot in the present. So this leaves us with the cost side and the costs are real, so how can we prevent them from becoming tangible? This question inspired behavioural economist Richard Thaler to come up with an innovative and successful mechanic for company employees to fund their pensions, called the 'Save More Tomorrow' plan. The subscriber doesn't pay anything until their next pay rise. A certain amount of the increase is automatically transferred into the pension fund. Objectively, it is the same outcome for the employee but the experience is very different. First, there is no direct signal for cost; rather, the signal that is perceived is 'more money', i.e. value. Second, the employee does not have to give away something they have already received (i.e. 'own'). This significantly reduces perceived pain. Additionally, by postponing future additional payments (because they are linked only to the occasion of the next pay rise), the costs are discounted by this temporal distance. So overall, by using the principles of tangibility, immediacy and certainty, the barriers were reduced, thereby increasing the net value of the decision.

Suggestion

Use all three principles (tangibility, immediacy and certainty) to optimize your decision interfaces.

Heuristics work internationally

There's another aspect that makes implicit decision rules so attractive for marketers: they work internationally. As marketers, we often face the challenge that we need to manage international brands, finding the right balance between scale efficiency and regional focus. Do decision interfaces and the heuristics they implement work internationally? Looking at this question, researchers in a study tried to understand better how sales can be influenced by the structure of an offer. They used the example of ordering pizza in both the US and Italy. Consumers were asked to either build up from a base product by adding extra toppings (i.e. the default was no toppings), or to scale down from a fully loaded product by subtracting toppings (where the default was many toppings) – see Figure 4.13. In both

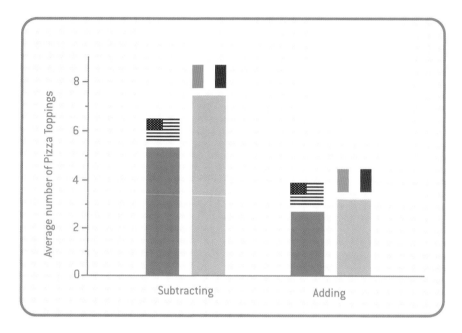

Figure 4.13 Decision rules work internationally

countries consumers ended up with twice as many ingredients when required to remove items from the offer instead of adding them. This, of course, means higher revenue and profit for the seller.

In a related study, consumers presented with a 'fully loaded' car and given the opportunity to remove optional features in order to save money ended up with a more expensive set of features than those presented with a basic model and given the opportunity to add features. Adding or subtracting features or toppings are both highly perceivable processes but with very different effects. Adding focuses attention on increasing the price, whereas subtracting is all about reducing the costs. The marketing implications of this are clear. Starting with a large number of components or features and allowing consumers to scale down from there leads to the acceptance of a higher-priced product than starting with a basic product and asking consumers to build up from it.

The pizza study reveals another interesting finding that holds true for almost all heuristics: they work in every country and every culture. The automatic decision rules we are looking at in this chapter are grounded in the way human perception works, and therefore should be similar, if not identical, for most populations. It is safe to assume that all humans are loss averse – this makes sense from an evolutionary perspective. Framing effects have been found around the world. The true influence of cultural learning on decoding happens at another, more semantic level of processing. It is when the autopilot asks the 'what does it stand for?' question, where culture comes in much more strongly, and where we find significant differences across cultures. Developing international campaigns is hard, because the signals that are used, like testimonials, symbols or colours, can have different meanings in the various cultures. While it may be successful to use a purple cow as a symbol for a chocolate product in Germany, France or the UK, it is probably not a great idea to use this visual in India, where a cow is a religious icon. However, because heuristics are highly automated and deeply grounded in the way perception works, they do provide opportunities that can be exploited across countries and cultures.

This completes our tour d'horizon across the key learnings of implicit decision rules and heuristics as applied to optimizing touchpoints. A key question remains unanswered, however: what drives people to visit, for example, Groupon.com in the first place? What is the underlying motivation? Clearly there is more to purchase decisions than tangibility, immediacy and certainty of rewards. These principles significantly increase the likelihood of a sale once people visit an interface, but what makes them visit in the first place? Fiat can increase conversion with its 'pay 50 per cent two years later' promotion, but what makes people consider Fiat as a brand? And why do people want a car anyway? To answer this we need to look into another key driver of purchase decisions: the goals consumers pursue when buying products and services.

What we have learned in this chapter

- Decision interfaces change behaviour without changing minds. This behaviour change subsequently changes attitudes.
- Because autopilot processing is heavily influenced by perception, the experienced net value is affected by the signals consumers perceive through their senses. Everything else is just claimed and will not have an impact on the autopilot.
- We can influence decision making through decision interfaces by using three meta-principles: tangibility, immediacy and certainty.

What this means to us as marketers

- Through the signals we use at the decision interface we can directly influence behaviour and hence purchases without an intermediate step of changing consumer attitudes. This complements the typical approach for non-interactive touchpoints (e.g. broadcast media) where the focus is, broadly, on attitude change.
- To maximize the persuasiveness of marketing, a key question is: how can we convert touchpoints into decision interfaces? In other words, how can we turn the consumer from being a passive observer of a touchpoint (e.g. a TV ad) into an active decision maker?
- Perception and experience are all there is, so our value propositions need to be perceivable and experienceable through the senses, otherwise the impact on the autopilot will be severely compromised.

5

Goals

The Driving Forces of Purchase Decisions

To fully understand purchase behaviour we need to understand what motivates people to buy products and brands in the first place. Why do we buy what we buy? To answer this question we will introduce the concept of goals. Goals are a hot topic in psychology and neuroscience. Goal-based valuation is the most sophisticated level of value in the human brain, and it is a key concept in our journey to answer the question of why we buy what we buy. This chapter shows how powerful and valuable the concept of goals is for marketing.

Goal value – the driver of motivated behaviour

We have seen the many powerful ways to optimize interfaces along the path to purchase. Using insights from behavioural economics there are fascinating possibilities to add value and reduce cost. We can use heuristics to optimize our tariff structures, flyers and promotions when selling, for example, cars. But why does someone want to buy a car in the first place? And from which brands will they seek information? There clearly is an additional level that drives the value–cost equation, above and beyond heuristics, and this level is motivation. Motivation is the main driving force behind all human behaviour and, hence, purchase behaviour, so let's have a closer look at what motivation is about from a neuropsychological perspective.

A fascinating paper called 'A neural predictor of cultural popularity' (2012) by Gregory Berns and Sara Moore from Emory University sheds some light on the nature of motivated choice. They used fMRI to measure the brain response of a group of adolescents who were listening to songs of relatively unknown artists. After the brain scanning was completed, they asked respondents to rate their liking of the songs. The goal of this research was to identify the predictors of future sales, so the sales of these songs were totalled for the three years following the brain scans. The researchers then identified the neural predictor of sales by correlating the brain response with the actual sales. So which brain areas are most predictive of future sales?

We have already encountered the study by Brian Knutson *et al.* (2007) which showed that activation in the brain's reward centre predicts purchases within individuals, under a certain level of pain induced by price. The question Berns and Moore (2012) investigated was whether the same reward-based mechanism could also predict purchase decisions of the population at large. Indeed, they found that there was a significant correlation between activation in the reward system (OFC, ventral striatum) and future sales – the songs which elicited a high activation of the reward system enjoyed significantly higher sales compared with songs that did not activate this system. While activity in the reward centre was significantly correlated with the number of units sold, the subjective likability of the songs was not predictive of sales. In the words of Berns and Moore: 'This indicates that simple subjective reports of focus groups may not be good predictors of commercial success.'

It has been known for a while that wanting and liking are regulated by different neural circuits in the brain. We also experience this in our own lives. We like the old bookstore around the corner, but we buy our books from Amazon. Drug addicts repeatedly inject themselves with morphine, although the injection is painful. The reason for this is that there are different circuits in the brain for 'liking' and 'wanting'.

So if wanting and reward expectations drive purchase behaviour rather than liking, we would expect reward to also be the key driver of our willingness to pay for a product. Indeed, that is what many recent neuro-economic studies have found. Willingness to pay is a central parameter in neuro-economic research since it addresses the core of economics: why do people buy products and brands? A study in 2008 by three leading neuro-economists, Antonio Rangel, John O'Doherty and Hilke Plassmann, monitored hungry people in a brain scanner during an auction in which the respondents had to place bids (in dollars) in order to get items. Some of the items in the auction were non-food, while others were food items such as a candy bar. The key result was that the reward centre in the OFC determines willingness to pay for the food items. Hungry participants were willing to pay more for a food item because the hungry brain evaluated the food item as more rewarding, and this was based on increased activation in the OFC. For satiated participants the food items were less rewarding and hence they were less willing to pay, corresponding to much lower activations in the OFC. It appears plausible that if we are hungry, and therefore have the goal to eat, we associate high value with a product that fits this active goal and this, in turn, increases our willingness to pay. This experiment is interesting because it uncovers the basic principle that drives willingness to pay: the more relevant a product or service is for an active goal, the higher the expected reward and the more we are prepared to pay. Neuroscientists call this the *goal value*.

Goal-based valuation is the most sophisticated level of value in the human brain. Thanks to the new brain-imaging techniques and clever psychological experiments, the core principles of this critical level of valuation have been decoded. Products and brands offer a high goal value and so consumers have a high willingness to pay when they fit with their goals. It is only thanks to this universal currency of goal value that our brain is able to decide which of two completely unrelated things, such as a new car or a spa break, we want to invest our money in, or to decide which of two competing brands we prefer. Of course, we don't always have consistent active goals in every situation. At work we strive for achievement and recognition, whereas at home, harmony and companionship are more important. We have one lipstick to meet the goal of 'care' and another for 'attractiveness'. We have different active goals when choosing a car than we do when buying washing powder or toothpaste. The way the brain derives the final decision is by establishing a relative ranking of the options based on their relative goal value. It then chooses the one with the highest overall goal value specific to the given context. This explains why some consumers consider purchasing our brand but, in the end, do not. Our product in this case offers good goal value, but not the best. This is what neuro-economists refer to as the 'winner takes all' effect. Only the number one brand in the consumer's goal ranking will be chosen. It is not sufficient to be in the relevant consideration set; it is important for a brand to be number one regarding specific occasions, as we saw with the ice-cream example in Chapter 2, or regarding a specific reward such as security in the automotive category.

The calculations of goal value and willingness to pay – no matter whether it is food, music, services or cars – are mainly processed in the reward centre (OFC, ventral striatum). Renowned psychologist Art Dijksterhuis, author of *The Smart Unconscious*, refers to goals as 'mental representations of behaviours or behavioural outcomes that are rewarding'. Based on experience and expectations, our brain calculates the extent to which a product fits with, and helps to achieve, our goals.

The 'winner takes all' effect: consumers choose the product with the highest fit to their dominant goal in a given situation.

The nature of motivated behaviour is to achieve goals that are of high value for us. We go to university because we want a career. We become a punk rocker because we want to rebel against the establishment. We embark on a safari in South Africa because we want excitement. If we are hungry, food has a high goal value, motivating us to drive to a supermarket or to search for the nearest McDonald's restaurant. If we leave a restaurant full up after a meal then the next restaurant we pass on our way home will no longer have any goal value. The effects of a lack of goal value become visible in people with depressive disorders: their brain is not able to apply any goal value to anything. They don't even eat or get out of bed. Nothing is motivating for them any more.

What does this mean for marketing? Goals are the key concept to understand why we buy what we buy. We buy drinks in order to quench our thirst. We buy detergents in order to clean our clothes and we choose Ariel because we want to be a good housewife. We purchase a car because we want to drive from A to B and we choose the Volvo brand because we want to do that in the safest possible way. Others have the goal to show off their wealth and therefore they drive a Porsche or buy a Rolex for thousands of pounds. No matter what we do, no matter in which area of our life, our goals determine what we do. This is highlighted in the following quotation from Roy D'Andrade, a well-known anthropologist:

> To understand people one needs to understand what leads them to act as they do, and to understand what leads them to act as they do one needs to know their goals.

Products and brands are instruments with which consumers achieve goals. In the words of the famous Harvard Professor Theodore Levitt: 'People don't want to buy a quarter-inch drill – they want a quarter-inch hole!' In a brilliant *Harvard Business Review* article with the telling title 'Marketing malpractice: the cause and the cure' (2009), Marketing Professor Clayton M. Christensen from Harvard University refers to this requirement as the *job* for which a product is 'hired' by consumers. When people have a job that needs doing, when they have a goal that they want to achieve, they hire products to do that job for them. As marketers, we therefore need to create product experiences that deliver these consumer goals.

As simple as this may seem, asking the question 'what is the goal, what is the job that consumers want to get done?' has significant impact on how we think of markets, how we segment the market and how we deal with product development, as illustrated by the following example from the Clayton Christensen article (2009).

A fast-food restaurant wanted to increase sales of their milkshakes by improving the product. Initially they followed the standard approach: they defined the market using the product category of 'milkshakes' and segmented consumers by demographics and personality characteristics. They then researched among these segments to find out which product features were desired (e.g. thicker or chunkier) and at which price point consumers would buy. Unfortunately, the resulting improvements did not have any impact on sales.

The goal perspective changed the way the problem was approached. Trying to find out for which job the consumer wanted a milkshake, the company analyzed purchase behaviour and the situational context in which purchase and consumption occurs. Through studying actual behaviour they discovered that a milkshake meets different goals. One goal is to consume milkshake as a filling snack to help pass the time (relieve boredom). This goal-based segment purchases milkshakes in the morning, usually on their own, and consumes the shake during a long drive to work. When questioned about potential substitutes in this given situation, these consumers revealed that they sometimes eat bagels or doughnuts instead. They reported that they are not hungry at the time of purchase but wanted to prevent hunger before lunchtime. A milkshake does this job better than the substitutes – because it is thick, it takes a long time to consume and therefore consumption lasts the entire journey. Sucking it through a straw has a playful element and consuming it in the car is convenient.

The research identified another goal segment: using milkshakes as a dessert. Parents purchased the milkshake for their children. Observation revealed that this purchase includes high behavioural costs for the parents as it takes the children quite a long time to suck the milkshake through a thin straw. This long duration does not fit with the overall context of going to a fast-food restaurant with the kids. In summary, the company discovered two very different goal segments, hence two different jobs for which people 'hired' milkshake.

The goal segments provide clear guidelines for product improvement and also identify the sweet spots that communication needs to trigger in order to increase sales. To best deliver the goal of having a filling snack to pass the time, the shake needs to be thick and straws should be thin. Also, including an element of surprise (e.g. some chunky ingredients) will help to alleviate boredom. However, in order to best deliver the goal of being purchased as a dessert for children, the shake needs to be able to be consumed fast. Previous research lacked specificity regarding the job each individual consumer had in mind when buying a milkshake. This resulted in suggestions for product improvements that averaged out to a 'one size fits none' requirement (e.g. some wanted a thicker product, others wanted it thinner). Merely using socio-demographics and personality characteristics, they were not able to distinguish between the two goal segments, leading to product development requirements that served neither of the two goal segments sufficiently.

This is a key reason for failed innovations: they are often not focused on improving a specific goal value, i.e. how well the job is done. Using the goals that are dominant in a given situation as the main frame of reference, marketing can trigger wanting (and hence purchases) instead of liking.

The consumer goal – not the customer or the category – is the fundamental unit from which to define the market, to inspire successful new product development and to develop marketing strategies. Products have a high goal value when they do the job better than any other product specific to a given situation.

This milkshake case has another important implication: the consumer goal – the job that needs to be done – defines the market and with it the true competition against which we need to achieve an advantage. The underlying principle in our brain is what's termed 'goal-based categorization'. Imagine we have a doughnut, an apple and an orange in front of us. If we are asked to group the products that are healthy, we would create a category consisting of the apple and the orange. However, grouping them using the goal of a quick snack would result in a category consisting of the doughnut and the apple. How consumers group products will depend on the current goal they want to achieve. In the above case of milkshakes, the competition is not just other milkshakes but also bananas, doughnuts and bagels, for example. Thinking of goals or of the job to be done in a given situation changes our view of the market and of the real competition, and unlocks opportunities as well as growth potential. In the words of Christensen (2009):

Job-defined markets are generally much larger than product category-defined markets. Marketers who are stuck in the mental trap that equates market size with product categories don't understand whom they are competing against from the customer's point of view.

Goals drive attention

If motivated behaviour is driven by goals that are currently active, it appears only logical that goals act as the core criteria that the brain uses to filter incoming signals. We already came across the example of how we perceive the world when we are hungry – we focus more on food-related signals such as a McDonald's logo. Our autopilot scans the environment and matches the incoming signals with our goals. If our goal is to buy an energizing shower gel, our autopilot is tuned to look for signals in the environment which promise to fulfil this goal. When we spot some packaging that resembles motor oil and which carries the name 'Dynamic Pulse', the match is high and we turn our attention towards this product. In other words, goals determine our attention – we notice things if they signal high goal value. This is, in itself, not a new finding – Russian psychologist Alfred Yarbus examined how goals control our attention more than 40 years ago. In a classic piece of psychological research he asked people with different goals in mind to look at a picture. One task, for example, was to determine the age of the people depicted. At the same time, he measured where people were looking (via eye tracking). Figure 5.1 shows that, depending on the goal, people paid attention to very different things in the picture. If the goal was to find out something about the family's material circumstances, people paid more attention to the pictures on the wall. If, however, the task was to guess the age of the people present, people's faces became the focus.

Goals also determine attention when we look at press advertising, as a study by marketing professors Rik Pieters and Michel Wedel shows. Their conclusion from a variety of experiments is as follows:

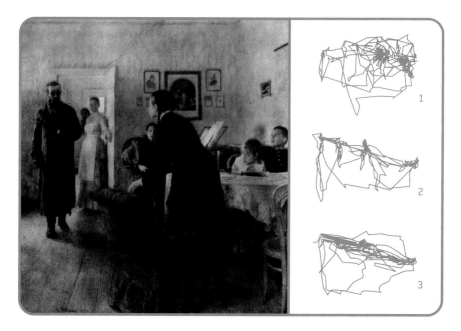

Figure 5.1 Goals drive attention in a classic experiment by Russian psychologist Alfred Yarbus. Eye tracking is shown specific to the tasks: (1) 'Evaluate the family's material circumstances', (2) 'Guess the ages of all persons present', (3) 'Assess how long the visitor had been away from the family'.

The results of this study show the fast and systematic influence which goals have on visual attention of advertising. Furthermore, this study shows that the information content of advertising is dependent on the goals which customers have during the observation. Despite consumers observing the average advert for only 4 seconds, their goals determined the length of observation of brand, picture and copy text.

How goal-based attention works is shown in more detail by a recent study by Julia Vogt from Ghent University in Belgium. The study investigated whether current goals bias attention towards stimuli that represent the means by which the goal can be achieved and, therefore, those stimuli which have high goal value. The scientists induced disgust by getting participants to touch fake revolting objects such as a plastic cockroach placed on a biscuit or plastic faeces. Participants in the control cell touched objects that were not revolting. The results of a subsequent test assessing attention to a range of pictures revealed that attention of those exposed to disgusting stimuli was oriented towards pictures representing cleanliness, such as hands holding some soap, or water droplets falling into water. The cleanliness pictures had high goal value for participants in the disgust-induced condition and so their autopilot allocated more attention to them. The key learning is that the products that promise to do the job best get the biggest share of attention. To achieve stand-out of our ads and impact on shelf we have to understand the goals consumers try to achieve with our product and brand since goal value will be a key driver of the amount of attention allocated.

A common key performance indicator (KPI) in marketing is for the brand to be top of mind. That is, the brand should be number one if consumers are asked which brand comes to mind when they think of a certain category (e.g. which brand comes to mind if you think of cars). Goal-based attention implies that the brand that springs to mind will depend on the consumer's active goals. If we think of a car that best fits the goal of a joyful driving experience, different brands will come to mind compared with when we think of a car for status, or a car for security. So goals can activate brands in our memory, and this is important for positioning and strategy work. Instead of asking with which properties the brand is associated, we can (e.g. in tracking) ask which goals activate the brand. In other words, how salient is the brand as a means to attain the goal in a specific given buying situation?

Byron Sharp, director of the Ehrenberg-Bass Institute for Marketing Science, writes: 'Attitudes are about evaluating the brand (do you think it is a good brand?), whereas salience is largely about having a chance of being thought of (are you likely to notice or retrieve the brand in that buying situation?).'

The autopilot implicitly matches signals in the environment with goals that are currently active. As a result of this matching, attention is allocated to the signal which shows the highest fit to the active goals.

For positioning work this confirms that, in order to be both relevant and differentiating, we need to link our brand to a relevant goal that is not yet owned by another brand.

Implicit goal pursuit: goals can be activated and monitored on autopilot

Considering the huge number of decisions we make every day, let's understand better how our brain accomplishes all this goal management. The term 'goal' initially sounds like we might make a decision only after reflection and having thought things through thoroughly. Subjectively, however, we don't feel as if we decide through lots of deliberation and mulling things over. We don't think about our career goal every minute of the day, or even every minute we are at work. In most cases we act intuitively, in autopilot mode. Indeed, recent research shows that goals can be activated and monitored at an implicit level, something neuropsychologists call 'implicit goal pursuit'.

Just how this implicit goal pursuit in the autopilot works is shown in the following study. It makes use of the fact that money has a high goal value because, as consumers, we've learned that we can achieve many goals with it. Participants were asked to complete several tasks and were shown on a screen how much money they could earn if they completed each task correctly. If the reward for accomplishing the task was only €0.05, then the participants worked less hard than during the tasks for which the reward was €1. This is not surprising. However, this differing response to the reward was also confirmed by implicit reactions, such as the widening of pupils and other physiological reactions. Even more surprisingly, the goal of achieving the monetary reward was activated even when researchers displayed the monetary reward on the screen for such a short time that participants could not consciously perceive it. The core information of whether the amount of money was high or low was registered implicitly by the autopilot, which in turn set off the same level of goal pursuit and corresponding physiological reactions as the conscious perception of the monetary amount did.

In another study, participants who were habitual or non-habitual bicycle riders were subtly primed with the goal of travelling (around town). They then completed a task that measured the accessibility of the word bicycle (i.e. how easily the word springs to mind). The results showed that among those who had first been implicitly primed with a travel goal, habitual bike riders showed enhanced accessibility to the word bicycle compared with non-habitual bike riders. Interestingly, habitual and non-habitual bike riders did not differ in the accessibility of the word bicycle when the travel goal had not been primed. This demonstrates that for people who have repeatedly used a particular means to meet a goal, such as riding one's bike in order to get from point A to point B, corresponding information can become more accessible in memory after the goal has been primed. This is why it matters how we ask which brand is top of mind – the stronger the goal–brand link, the more likely the brand will be top of mind once the goal is activated (even if the goal is activated on an implicit level).

Implicitly activated goals not only make products or brands more accessible, they also result in a more positive attitude. In a series of experiments, participants were implicitly primed with words relevant to a goal (e.g. achievement, dieting, cooperation) and then completed an implicit attitude measure. The results showed that those primed with the goal exhibited significantly more positive implicit attitudes towards those stimuli that were highly relevant and helpful to achievement of the goal. For example, those implicitly primed with the goal 'to be slim' displayed significantly more positive implicit attitudes towards 'gym' and 'salad'.

In another study on implicit goal pursuit, participants read a short story about a guy trying to pick up a woman in a bar. The authors expected that, among the male participants, this would activate the goal to seek casual sex. Participants were then asked to provide feedback on a computer task to either a male or female experimenter. Those who were primed with the short story were significantly more helpful to the female experimenter (but not to the male) than those not primed. Critically, there was no difference between those in the primed condition and those in the unprimed condition in terms of their awareness of being helpful, suggesting that the goal was influencing their behaviour towards the female experimenter in a subtle, implicit manner.

For a long time, it was generally assumed that many of the mental processes that make goal pursuit possible require conscious awareness. But in the past decade or so, the scientific study of goal pursuit has discovered that these processes can also operate without conscious awareness. In a paper published in *Science* in 2010, Psychology Professors Ruud Custers and Henk Aarts from Utrecht University summarize this research as follows:

> *A large body of research indicates that the pursuit of goals can be evoked outside of awareness. People become motivated to initiate and exhibit behaviours available in their repertoire when goals that are represented as desired outcomes are primed, even though they are not aware of the primed goal or its effect on their motivation and behaviour.*

Goals can be activated and pursued on autopilot.

We will have a closer look at implicit goals later in this chapter, as they play a crucial role in marketing.

Relevance – purchase as a means to an end

The more important the goal, the higher the value and willingness to pay and, hence, the greater the relevance of a product. Let's use again the example of Dynamic Pulse shower gel from Adidas. This shower gel is relevant for people seeking to recharge their batteries and get a kick start in the shower. The product clearly does not signal a fit with the goal of relaxation, however, therefore it is much less relevant if relaxation rather than recharging is the dominant goal. So if we are at the shower gel fixture, we will pay most attention to, and more likely buy, the one with the highest fit to our active goals when taking a shower.

Goal achievement underlies what we call relevance in marketing.

A study by Colorado University shows this principle at work. Participants were asked to decide between two different plant fertilizers. One group was instructed to choose the product they perceived to be the easiest to use, i.e. with the goal of less effort. The other group was told to choose the product they thought would best achieve the growth of healthy green plants, i.e. with the goal of better results. The products differed only in the description of product usage. One description matched the goal of less effort (e.g. 'Use one half to one cup of fertilizer'), the other matched the goal of better results (e.g. 'Use half a cup for plants up to 30cm and a full cup for all plants bigger than this'). So, does it make a difference if the product description matches the customer's goal? The results are very clear: 82 per cent of those with the goal of 'minimum effort' chose the product with the matching description. For those whose goal it was to achieve better results, a staggering 90 per cent chose the product with the description that matched their goal.

In a study undertaken by the University of Toronto, participants were asked to recall and write down situations in which they were socially excluded, for example when they were not allowed to join in playing football at school or when they were the only person not invited to a party. Another group in the experiment was asked to make a note of situations when they were with good friends, for example on a holiday together. After the participants had thought about their appropriate social memories and had written them down, they were offered a choice of different products under the pretext of offering them some refreshment.

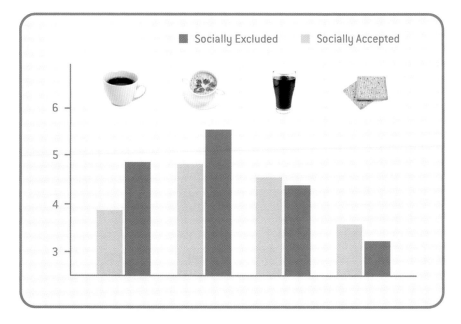

Figure 5.2 An experiment from Chen-Bo Zhong and Jeffrey Leonardelli (2008) shows social exclusion increases the desire for something warm. Images courtesy of Shutterstock

The choices were a Coke, a cracker, a coffee or a soup. The researchers were interested in whether the two different social experiences would influence the choice of product.

The mere recollection of a social situation had obviously affected the choice of product. Why? It's not a coincidence, so what is happening here? Let's consider what soup and coffee have in common. One attribute common to these two products is their temperature: unlike Coke and a cracker, they are both warm. This would appear to be more influential in the choices made than the taste of each product. At first glance this seems strange – what could possibly be the connection between the physical characteristic of 'warmth' and social exclusion? How come, if they felt socially excluded, they opted for a hot drink? Physical temperature has affective consequences, because being held close to a loving caregiver as an infant is also associated with bodily contact with a warm object, namely another human being. The link between social inclusion and warmth originates in childhood, and becomes imprinted in our brains through the 'what fires together wires together' learning rule. We can also see this connection in everyday life when we talk, for example, of 'warm-hearted' people, or others to whom we don't 'warm' because we view them as 'cold'. So, what happened is that the task of recalling moments when participants felt socially excluded prompted a goal (i.e. to compensate for the 'social coldness' they felt) that could be better addressed through the choice and consumption of a warm soup or coffee than by the alternative products that don't offer such 'warmth'. The 'socially excluded' participants had an additional goal in mind when choosing their refreshment – to compensate for the 'lack of warmth' they felt owing to the effect of the task they had just completed.

This experiment shows that the participants' choice of product was specific to achieving their goals. It is safe to assume that they all liked crackers and cola but these did not fit to the goal that was dominant and hence were not chosen. The respondents' goal was to reduce the discomfort they had felt by being socially excluded and so they chose products that were best able to address the goal of social inclusion, the products that offered warmth. This ability of products to bring us closer to our goals – even if only symbolically as in this case – is called *instrumentality*.

Brands and products are means to an end and this instrumentality to achieve goals is their true motivational power. We 'hire' products as an instrument to get the job done.

Brands serve consumer goals

Many brand positioning statements contain values such as 'sympathy', 'reliability', 'trust' or 'authenticity'. If, however, brands are a means to an end, then we must ask ourselves whether people really buy personality traits from brands. Is 'sympathy' really a goal we want to achieve with a brand? Do we see different brands as different people? Can our relationship with brands be seen as an interpersonal one?

The question of whether our brain sees brands as people or objects can be answered in a straightforward way. It is known which brain areas are activated when we see and judge people. It is also known that objects (e.g. a car or toothbrush) are processed in a different region of the brain. There is, therefore, a clear distinction between objects and people in the brain. This seems plausible as well. So does the brain treat brands like objects or like people?

A neuroscientific study at Michigan University, led by Marketing Professor Carolyn Yoon (2006), looked at just that. Participants in a brain scanner saw brands that they knew and used (e.g. Apple, McDonald's) as well as other brands that they knew but didn't use. On top of that, the names of well-known people such as Bill Clinton were displayed along with the participant's own name. Brands and names were presented together with a multitude of adjectives from a standard test of brand evaluation, e.g. 'reliable', 'honest', 'likable' or 'jolly'. The participants were asked to indicate, by pushing a button, whether or not an adjective fitted a brand or a person. At the same time, readings were taken of their brain activity.

The result was very clear. When participants judged people (whether celebrities or themselves), this activated the medial part of the frontal lobe. It is known that this brain region reacts to people. What happened with the brands? They activated an area that is known to react to physical objects. Brands are objects to the brain; they do, after all, belong to physical objects and businesses. From the brain's point of view, therefore, brands are not people with personality traits. Concluding their study, Carolyn Yoon's research team wrote: 'These results cast doubt on the view that products and brands are like people.'

Of course, we form a relationship of sorts with brands, but only in the sense of the degree to which a brand enables us to achieve a goal. The more important the goal is to us, the stronger we relate to the brand in question. That doesn't mean, though, that the brain treats brands like people. We only buy products and services because we want to be able to do something, to be or become something or to have something. We do not purchase a body lotion because we want to be or become authentic, or reliable or sympathetic. So if, in marketing, we start to use the sentence 'By purchasing the brand/product our customers want to be, have, do . . .' and we fill in our brand values, we can easily check whether or not our positioning is a goal-based value positioning.

Suggestion

Looking at the words in your strategic papers, e.g. the brand values, which of them are goals that consumers want to achieve with the product?

After all, we don't want to go for coffee with a brand, as we would with a friend or acquaintance. Brands are means to an end and this is the nature of the relationship we have with brands. Even if brands are used as extensions of our self, we still use them to achieve a goal – to signal to the world and ourselves who we are, what we have or what we do. If we are a supporter of Greenpeace, by wearing a Greenpeace t-shirt we signal that we are responsible and concerned about sustainability.

An experiment by Duke University demonstrates that brands are indeed linked to goal achievement and that goals can be activated and monitored at an implicit level.

The nature of the relationship between consumer and brand is not that of an interpersonal relationship. Customers do not buy a brand's personality traits but its expected instrumentality to achieve a certain goal.

Under the pretext of an eye test, participants were placed in front of a monitor. They were shown pictures and had to decide whether the picture could be seen on the left- or right-hand side, while adding up numbers at the same time. This ensured that their (limited) pilot system was at full capacity. Immediately before showing the pictures, the researchers displayed brand logos, but for such a short period of time that they could only be processed implicitly in the autopilot. There were two matched participant groups in this study – one was exposed to the IBM logo, the other to the Apple logo.

Immediately afterwards, participants were asked to perform a creativity test. They were asked, for example, to spontaneously name possible uses for a brick, other than its usual role in the building of a wall. So a brick could be used as a paperweight, or as a hammer. The astonishing result was that those participants who had seen the Apple logo came up with significantly more ideas than those who had seen the IBM logo. Additionally, the ideas from the Apple group were rated by an independent jury as being much more creative. So if, when choosing a computer to purchase, our goal is to be creative (or to be seen as creative), the Apple computer is the right choice. If, however, our goal is to be efficient, then an IBM might fit better with our goal. Additionally, this study shows that goals can be implicitly activated in, and implicitly managed by, the autopilot. The Apple logo changed the behaviour of participants, without them being aware of this process.

We buy expected goal achievement

Imagine we are an adolescent young man and we see the new Lynx/Axe advert where an average guy just like us turns into an attractive man for whom even angels leave heaven and drop down to earth. Because being attractive and getting desirable girls is certainly a valuable goal for us, we go out and buy the brand. However, when we use the body spray nothing really happens – no angels, no group of Amazonian women climbing a mountain to pursue us. Our disappointment should be huge, but it isn't. So if purchasing brands and products is about goal achievement, why do Lynx/Axe users continue to buy the product if the goal is not fulfilled? To answer this crucial question we need to have a closer look at how brands meet consumer goals.

Assume we want to eat a pot of yoghurt. Which step will activate our brain most strongly: seeing the container, picking it up, opening it, inserting the spoon and stirring the fruit, smelling it, eating the first spoonful, or eating the next? Most people we have asked choose inserting the spoon and stirring. In a study reported by A.K. Pradeep, CEO of science-based consumer-research company NeuroFocus, the yoghurt consumption process was tested using a brain-measurement technique. The result was that grasping and removing the foil covering the top of the container activates the consumer's brain most strongly across this whole process. More strongly than eating the first spoonful! This is in line with a lot of neuroscientific studies showing that the reward centre is triggered particularly strongly based on *expectations*. It is the rewards that we expect to get that drive valuation and hence motivate the purchase. This comes as no surprise, because if we calculate the goal value before we make the choice, we have to base this valuation on our expectations. Male youths using Lynx/Axe do not necessarily end up getting the most attractive girls, nor do they witness angels falling from the sky after spraying themselves with the product. However, they continue to buy and use the brand. They are not disappointed when it doesn't deliver exactly what the advertising suggests. The reason for this is that, through the campaign, the target audience builds an association between the usage of the product and the goal of being attractive to girls. This association makes the brand instrumental in achieving this goal. So if being noticed by girls is the dominant goal, this brand has the highest goal value compared with brands that are not as strongly associated with that goal (e.g. Sure/ Rexona).

Figure 5.3 The advert forms an association between the product and the goal of escapism

Now let's look at an advert for Bounty (see Figure 5.3). A woman sits on a lonely, rather desolate beach. She bites into a Bounty and the barren, isolated island begins to develop colourful, exotic and fantastic vegetation and finally an attractive man enters the scene.

No one believes that this actually happens when you eat a Bounty bar. It sounds like a fairytale, like a story. And that's exactly what it is. Brands create possibilities and offer fictitious, symbolic rewards that frame the physical effect of the product. The goal achievement therefore doesn't have to take place in reality because it takes place fictionally based on the established association between the brand usage and goal achievement.

The marketing world is full of examples analogous to these. A marketing expert at Harley-Davidson says: 'What we're selling is the possibility for a 43-year-old accountant to dress in black leather, drive through small villages and make other people fear him.'

We aren't actually able to keep going longer with a Snickers bar, but it sure feels like it. We aren't physically closer to our loved ones with a text message, but it feels like we are. The labels of strong alcoholic beverages should always be designed in a more traditional way, because strong drinks are rites of passage for the young and the labels help them to believe that they are reaching the next stage of developing into an adult. And by drinking, they are – on a symbolic level. These are the imaginings and possibilities that we associate with products and brands. Brands work implicitly in the background but develop a lasting effect on consumers' judgement and behaviour by activating expectations which, in turn, influence perceived and experienced value.

Consumers judge the value of a potential purchase based on expected goal achievement.

Brands work just like placebos. Just how strong these placebo or expectation-based effects can be is shown by a study involving aspirin. Study participants were told that they would be testing a new medicine for headaches to see whether it was better than medicines already on the market. As soon as participants developed a headache they were supposed to take two tablets and then note after one hour if, and by how much, their condition had improved. Some of the participants received the real aspirin tablets, the others were – unknowingly – given placebos. The placebo group received ineffective tablets but in original aspirin packaging. They believed, therefore, that they were taking real aspirin. The result? Simply because of the packaging the placebo tablets (which contained no active ingredient) reduced headaches significantly – not only reported pain relief but actual physiological reactions. The packaging with the aspirin logo on it activated expectations of pain relief which, in turn, changed neural activity patterns as if real aspirin were consumed. What this ultimately shows is how strong expectations effect physical reactions in humans. One expert in this field, Tor Wager from Columbia University, concludes that 'placebo is an active brain process with a substantial cognitive and evaluative component, not simply a reporting bias or passive adaptation'.

The same substance works twice as well if it is administered by injection rather than in tablet format – not for medical reasons but due to the increased expectations associated with injections. The colour of tablets also changes the physiological effect. Red pills – even if otherwise ineffective – raise blood pressure while blue ones lower it. Two ineffective red tablets work stronger than one due to the expectation that 'more helps more'. From the field of cancer research we also know that not only corrective effects but also side effects are caused by placebos. In a clinical study, patients were divided into a placebo group and a group which received the actual medication. Neither the doctors nor the patients knew who was in the placebo group (a so-called double blind experiment). Around 30 per cent of the placebo patients showed typical – i.e. expected – chemotherapy side effects, from feeling nauseous to being sick and experiencing hair loss, despite being injected only with a saline solution.

These expectation-based mechanisms are based on principles which are just as relevant to marketing. Participants in studies, who believed they had been given real coffee, showed an increased heart rate even when they had, in fact, been given decaffeinated coffee. A different study showed that the physiological effect of an energy drink reduced significantly when it was introduced at a discounted price – expectations of the drink's performance were lowered when the product was perceived as cheaper and this led to reduced effectiveness.

One key task in marketing is to build associations between the product, its usage and the achievement of a relevant goal. Through this consumers learn that the product has the ability to do the job, and why.

This also works in the opposite direction – seeing advertising about the effectiveness of the energy drink heightened its physiological impact, even though, objectively, there was no active ingredient (the product tested was just a placebo energy drink). Branding, pricing and other marketing activities that can create an expectation about how good an experience should be bias not only the perception of the consumption experience but also the processes in the brain with which this is correlated. For marketing management this implies that a certain level of product quality is important to ensure satisfied customers, but beyond that the expectation that a brand is able to trigger might be equally important.

Based on the developed capability of humans to achieve goals mentally and symbolically, we no longer need to fight each other in order to clarify who the alpha male is – we can buy a Rolex watch or a status-oriented Mercedes car to demonstrate this, and compete symbolically. This is less dangerous and less harmful! If we are in need of a warm hug, then we can consume a Batchelors Cup a Soup to help meet this goal. In each of these cases, it is sufficient that we expect the respective brand and product choice to be that which delivers best to help us achieve our dominant goal. We make these expectation judgements from everything that we have learned and experienced about the product or the brand.

How this works is shown in a study by British scientist Jay Gottfried of University College, London. Gottfried started by exposing his study subjects in a brain scanner to a pleasant scent, such as rose water, for ten seconds. A few seconds later, the participants each were shown a symbol: sometimes a helmet, a ball or a wooden chest. Their task, within the next few seconds, was to think up a short story which creatively linked the scent of roses to a helmet, for example. Then came the next scent, a new symbol and a further made-up short story. It was only after a learning phase with around 130 different symbols and nine changing smells that the actual memory test started. For this purpose, Gottfried mixed old symbols with new ones. The subjects were asked to recall which symbols they had already been shown.

The result was surprising. Whenever participants recognized a symbol that they had seen previously, the brain area which actually responds to scents also lit up in the scanner, despite the fact that no more smells were released during this testing phase. A sort of 'virtual' smell emerged based on the association that had been built before. Like a self-fulfilling prophecy, the learned associations created the expected experience. So the same principle that we came across when consumers 'tasted' chocolate pudding because of the brown colour (although it was actually vanilla pudding) applies for the goal value as well: we experience what we expect.

Across our marketing practices we often encounter symptoms of these expectation-based mechanisms. For example, in advertising tracking, how often are there respondents who recall certain advertising for a brand that hasn't been on air for years, even decades? As an example, 'chimps' advertising for the PG Tips tea brand hasn't been aired for more than 15 years, but this is often cited in recent studies. Consumers believe that they have 'seen' it because they expect to see it. Our expectations are based on memory, on everything that we have learned. So when questioned (and hence prompted) it is easy to respond in line with our expectations, and not with our factual experience.

The two levels of goal value

We have now seen that the main driver of the value side of the value–cost equation is the goal value of a brand. With this in mind, let's consider once more the Dynamic Pulse shower gel from Adidas. For this product to be relevant, it needs to fit the goals of consumers. The relevant goals in this case are, among others, scent, moisturization and care for skin. Meeting these goals qualifies a product to compete in the market. But they are hardly differentiating – every successful shower gel brand has these associations to some extent. However, by using signals that are associated with masculinity and energy (the motor-oil packaging codes), this product increases its perceived value.

We can understand the reason for this better now. By sending these signals the product tells the autopilot that, besides the generic category goals, we can achieve the additional, more psychological goal of getting energized. This symbolic level of goal value increases the net value for those consumers whose dominant goal is to be energized. This can, of course, vary, and not only across consumers – even the same consumer can have different dominant goals depending on their situation. For the morning shower, energizing is a popular dominant goal, but in the evening, an indulgent, more caring shower gel has higher goal value because we want to indulge ourselves after a tough day at work.

Let's look at another example. Although the car maker has had some recent issues, when you ask consumers why they would choose Toyota they claim that reliability is a key reason. However, if you ask those same consumers about a different car brand, they are likely to cite reliability, too. Besides meeting necessary (basic) factors such as reliability and quality, there need to be other differentiating goals to encourage consumers to choose a particular brand.

The advert in Figure 5.4 for Toyota Corolla tells us more about what the differentiating goal may be in the case of Toyota. Two friends are driving in a car on a country road. They see an attractive and alluringly dressed woman who is bent over the open bonnet of a car. The two men briefly look at each other expectantly. They approach the car and, just before stopping, the driver accelerates and keeps going. The passenger looks shocked and the driver says, with a confident smile, 'That was a trap; a Corolla doesn't break down'. And indeed we see that the attractive woman was, in fact, an ugly bald guy, angrily taking off a wig.

Figure 5.4 The advert explicitly communicates reliability and implicitly links the Toyota brand with being wise and sensible

185

Of course, the reliability goal is addressed in the ad, but there is another, more implicit aspect baked into this advert. The storyline includes the notion that the driver resists the temptation, is controlled, and acts reasonably. He resists the illusion. He is reasoned, wise and sensible. Toyota serves this psychological, implicit goal. Cars are obviously not only bought against the goal of driving from A to B, otherwise we would all drive a Reliant Robin! Cars are an extension of our identity and a symbol for what matters to us – mainly because our car is visible to others. Therefore, by driving a Toyota one can symbolically achieve the goal of being, or being seen as, wise and sensible. Other brands are objectively reliable as well, but this brand has the highest instrumentality to serve the additional, psychological goal of being sensible and resisting the 'bells and whistles' of other car brands. However, the goal value is high only for those for whom being sensible is the dominant goal. People who want to achieve the goal of fun or freedom with the purchase of a car will see little value in this advert and Toyota as a brand – they will see much more value in a Mini or a Jeep.

What these examples show is that when it comes to goals and goal value, there are two levels: explicit goals that are category specific (e.g. moisturizing our skin, reliability of a car, removing stains) and implicit goals that are more general and that operate on a psychological level (e.g. energizing, being sensible, fun or status). In marketing, we tend to focus a lot on the category-specific, explicit goals. But which body lotion doesn't claim to be nourishing? Which insurance company or utility provider doesn't have to be reliable, competent and reputable? The explicit goals are the reason why a product category emerges, so all competitors who want to survive in the market have to meet these goals.

When we ask consumers about brands and products, they will focus on the explicit goal level and talk about quality, reliability or price (even in the case of premium watches, as we have seen). The reason is, of course, that the implicit level operates in the background and does not come to the fore when we ask consumers such explicit questions. However, there is little difference between competitors at the explicit level, particularly in mature markets. In order to deliver the highest possible goal value and to provide relevant differentiation, we have to address the relevant implicit goals with our brands, products and communication. Stephen Brown, professor at the Kellogg School of Management, says: 'Just following consumer wishes leads to replaceable products, copycat advertising and stagnating markets.' Implicit goals run deeper than explicit consumer wishes and therefore can help to differentiate in a meaningful, relevant way.

As another example let's take Dove's 'natural beauty' campaign (see Figure 5.5). Natural beauty is a relevant proposition, but it is not distinctive. Body Shop offers natural beauty as well. So what is the distinctive goal value communicated by this campaign? Let's look at the brand signals more closely.

Figure 5.5 The Dove 'natural beauty' campaign connects the brand with the implicit goal of relief

To start with, the women were often shown in groups, so they weren't alone. The website contained pyjama party-like settings, which remind a woman of a time in her life when her hip size, cellulite and figure were not an issue. Dove helps in achieving the psychological goal of 'relief' – not the relief that one gets from a confession or from a pardon, but rather the relief from having to be constantly controlled or to optimize oneself. It's also a relief knowing that one is not alone with one's problem. Dove is like the old personal weighing scales that could be adjusted a little to make you feel better. The success of the campaign can therefore not just be traced back to showing normal women and authenticity.

There are two levels of jobs for which we can employ brands and products: to meet explicit goals that are category-specific, and to meet implicit goals that are more general and that operate at an underlying, psychological level.

This has been copied many times since but has usually not been as successful. Authenticity in itself is not a goal. It might make the brand likeable, but this alone doesn't lead to a purchase. This relief proposition was differentiating and relevant in the body care category when the campaign was launched. However, relief as a goal is much less relevant for categories such as cosmetics or hair care where the dominant goal is to transform and optimize, which helps explain why Dove has been much less successful in these categories.

The connection between explicit and implicit goals is not arbitrary: the product experience determines which implicit goals can be credibly linked to the explicit goal.

The connection between explicit and implicit goals is important. In the case of Bounty, the product experience is the basis for the implicit goal of escapism: chocolate with coconut. The associations we already have with coconut provide a credible bridge to the implicit goal of escapism – palm trees and desert islands. Likewise, the product's unique and luxurious texture and associated eating sensation also offer a credible link to the implicit goal. Contrast this with Snickers, for example, where you have to bite through nuts – a link to the implicit goal of escapism here is much less credible than one linking to a performance goal.

Decoding implicit goals

In order to increase relevance and hence willingness to pay, the key is to increase goal value on two levels: an explicit level which is specific to a given product category, and an implicit, psychological level which emerged long before products existed. This psychological level of goals is the key for developing differentiating propositions that go beyond the explicit goal value, yet it is much more challenging to capture systematically. For a start, we cannot simply ask consumers what it is. Fortunately, recent advances in affective neuroscience and the psychology of human motivation provide a robust and valid basis to systematically manage the implicit motivational level in order to develop differentiating and relevant propositions. Let's look at the most important learnings and how we can use them for marketing.

The two most basic motivational drives in our brain (next to the basics such as reproduction) are:

1. Promotion: approach, going forward, fighting, ascending, gain, etc.
2. Prevention: avoidance, protection, avoid-loss, etc.

These two motivational forces are deeply ingrained in us. They date back to ancient times when our choice for survival was either to fight (approach) or to take flight (avoidance). They are two sides of the same coin. If we want to attract users of shampoo for coloured hair we can address a promotive motivation by claiming that this shampoo makes the hair shine in brilliant colours. Or we claim the preventive proposition that this shampoo helps to avoid the loss of colour. Both propositions are possible. To maximize relevance, we have to know which focus is the most dominant one for the majority of customers.

189

Suggestion

When you think of your proposition and your competitors' propositions, do they have a preventive or promotive focus?

Let's take the example of a power drill. We use it to drill holes; this is our basic, explicit goal. A drill, however, serves additional, more implicit goals: it saves physical power and energy but most importantly it heightens the power and self-efficacy of the user (promotion goal). Power is the main implicit driver for the handyman: he can defeat hard concrete. The better performing and more powerful the machine, the more value for the user. So drills serve, as their implicit core, promotion goals. This proposition is nicely coded in the advert for Metabo power tools shown in Figure 5.6.

The headline is in German, yet we have no problem decoding the promotional goal being communicated: the drills are presented as weapons.

Figure 5.6 This advert addresses the implicit goal of power and self-efficacy

The headline supports this proposition: 'Concrete needs opponents, not victims.' An advert with a prevention focus would clearly look different. Knowing whether our consumers have a promotion or prevention focus has direct implications for the effectiveness of communication. Research shows that if consumers are promotion driven, executions of print ads that have a promotion focus are clearly more persuasive – and the other way around.

The two most basic motivational drivers are prevention and promotion.

Human motivation is, of course, more elaborate than just prevention and promotion. Various scientific disciplines, including affective neuroscience and the psychology of motivation, show that out of the rudimentary motivations of prevention and promotion, there developed what one might call the 'Big 3' human motivations that are grounded in physiological processes, operate deep within us and are universal in nature:

- **Security**: called *panic and fear system* in affective neuroscience, the goal of this system is to avoid fear and to strive for being cared for and for sociability (attachment, trust, togetherness, care, tradition, etc.). Brain evolution has provided safeguards to ensure that parents (usually the mother) take care of the offspring and the offspring have powerful emotional systems to indicate that they are in need of care (as reflected in crying or, as scientists prefer to say, 'separation calls'). This system is the motivational basis for many of the heuristics we saw in the previous chapter: loss aversion, social proof, status-quo bias, defaults. The main goals of this system are to avoid danger, avoid change, keep the status quo, avoid uncertainty, strive for stability and not waste energy.
- **Autonomy**: the *rage system* aims to avoid defeat and anger by being superior to others (e.g. status, performance). The goal ultimately is to be high in the hierarchy and to overcome resistance (power, performance, fight, etc.). A power drill serves this goal, as does an anti-ageing cream which promises transformation and beauty. Swiss

191

neuroscientist Walter Hess was awarded a Nobel Prize for analyzing this system in detail and showing that by stimulating certain subcortical brain areas in animals, rage could be triggered. One key hormone driving the rage system is testosterone. Studies show that when we win a match in, say, tennis, testosterone levels increase. The main goals of this system are to outperform others, assert yourself, increase your power and influence, expand your territory, get and stay in control.

- **Excitement**: the goal of the *seeking system* is to avoid boredom by seeking stimulation, change, innovation, etc. The motivation to play is closely related to this. From an evolutionary point of view the seeking system has evolved to motivate us to leave our home base to seek out, ultimately, new genes with which to mix. This system therefore is highly active during adolescence, strongly driving consumption goals (from drugs to fashion). The seeking system is based on dopamine, which is a key hormonal basis for learning. If an animal is given a lever that controls the onset of brain stimulation in this system, it will readily learn to push the lever and will eagerly continue to 'self-stimulate' for extended periods, until physical exhaustion and collapse set in. The main goals of the seeking system are to seek new and unfamiliar stimuli, break out of the familiar, discover and explore your environment, seek change, avoid boredom and be different from others.

Different strands of science independently confirm that these three are the key drivers of human behaviour. Each of these consists of a complex neural network including subcortical (i.e. very old) neural structures. They drive our behaviour from day one. Taking them one by one in turn, in the first few months of life, the proximity to parents, the security and the protection against danger are the most important things for a baby (security goal). The result is trust and attachment. A little later, when a child is crawling, and especially once it can walk, it begins to explore the environment on its own two feet. It wants to gain experience and try out different things. It is driven by curiosity (excitement goal). In doing this, it moves further and further from its mother and father. At this point, the child is already beginning to explore its boundaries and increase its independence from its parents (autonomy). At the very latest at preschool, it will start to fight over pecking orders; it is then driven by power and by prevailing. The excitement and autonomy systems reach their peak when we are around 20–30 years old, while the security system is at its peak both at the very beginning and towards the end of life.

Figure 5.7 captures what we have learned so far about basic human motivation systems. There is the basic distinction of promotion and prevention and, as we evolved, we built the more sophisticated 'Big 3' motivations upon them.

How do products and brands serve these implicit goals? Let's have a look. Metabo's power drill fulfils an autonomy goal by empowering the handyman. A different brand may frame its drill with excitement goals by focusing on the innovative features and the goal of creativity. Yet another brand

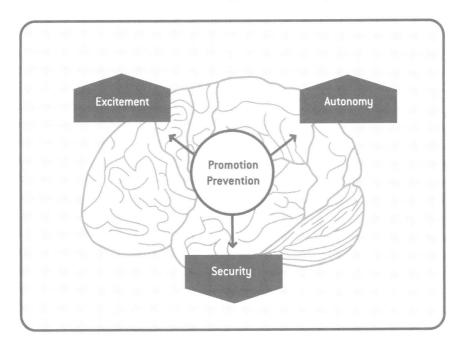

Figure 5.7 The basic implicit goal systems in the human brain

193

may stress its longevity and durability, and the solid materials with which the tool is produced, thereby addressing consumers with a more security-oriented goal. Volvo serves security goals through its safety framing, BMW is all about the joy of driving (excitement) and Mercedes addresses superiority and sovereignty (autonomy). Carlsberg is 'probably the best lager in the world' (autonomy), Carling taps into security (male camaraderie), while foreign beers such as Cobra or Tiger have their centre of gravity in the excitement domain (e.g. they are from 'exotic' countries like India).

In practice, it makes sense to supplement the three basic goal types by adding in their hybrid forms. Rock climbing, for example, is a mix between autonomy goals (getting to the top, performance, etc.) and excitement goals (vitality, fun, discovery). Wellness, meanwhile, is a mix of security goals (grooming, care, etc.) and excitement (stimulation with oils, massages, etc.). This results in a well-founded yet eminently manageable system of implicit goals that consists of a total of six motivational territories with which we are able to systematically think of implicit goals (see Figure 5.8):

- security: care, trust, closeness, security, warmth . . .
- enjoyment: relaxation, light heartedness, openness, pleasure . . .
- excitement: vitality, fun, curiosity, creativity, change . . .
- adventure: freedom, courage, rebellion, discovery, risk . . .
- autonomy: pride, success, power, superiority, recognition . . .
- discipline: precision, order, logic, reason . . .

People differ in which goal they want to achieve with a certain category. A Toyota driver regulates the discipline goal with this brand, but can use a Rolex watch to show his status (autonomy goal). Others do it the other way round – i.e. drive a Mercedes, but own and use a Sekonda sports watch. Since the implicit goals are universal and deeply ingrained in us, they can be served in many ways. We are very flexible in how we can achieve the implicit goals, because they are not grounded in a category like functional goals, they are grounded in basic human motivation. We

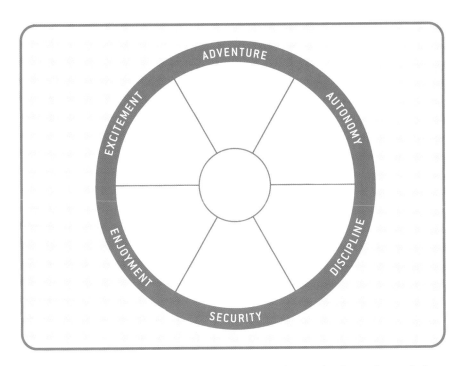

Figure 5.8 The *decode goal map*™ captures the implicit goals relevant for marketing

can use watches, cars, shoes or chairs to achieve an autonomy goal such as status. When we want to relax (enjoyment goal) we can take a short trip, go to yoga, visit a spa or use a shower gel that claims aromatherapy-like properties. As a consequence, one product category can address different goals. Ice cream can be a pragmatic choice for dessert (discipline). It can be linked to autonomy in the case of exclusive and sophisticated ice cream; it can help to achieve refreshment (excitement) or the goal of indulgence or escapism (adventure).

Suggestion

What is the dominant implicit goal with which your category or brand is associated? What other categories are used to achieve this goal?

195

In our consulting work we have used the decode goal map™ in hundreds of multinational projects, and across categories from detergents to cosmetics to telecommunications. One key learning from this work is that everyone intuitively understands the six dimensions because they reflect our core motivations, irrespective of whether we live in Mexico, India, Great Britain or wherever. Another key learning is that the map is complete in the sense that nothing important is missing when it comes to analyzing the motivational drivers of categories, brands and communication. A third learning is that it is very helpful to analyze, position and manage brands because, among other things, it can be linked with the specific, explicit goals of the product category.

Science has unlocked the basic human motivational drivers. This knowledge enables marketers to systematically manage this deep, implicit level of decision making.

Maximizing relevance and differentiation: goal-based brand propositions

There are many explicit and many implicit goals. Where should we start? We have to start with the explicit goal. This is the foundation of relevance. Without meeting these goals we would go out of business. And, most importantly, the brand that 'owns' the most important explicit goal is market leader. In the deodorant market the brand that is perceived to be superior in its explicit goal of protecting against sweat and odour is market leader. The brand in the fabric softener category that owns softness will be market leader. In marketing, we often focus on how we can differentiate and, as a result, we sometimes forget the basic, explicit goals of the category. The danger that lies in this approach is the possibility of forgetting the basic goal altogether and hence risking a lack of relevance.

The risk of not delivering at this level is demonstrated by the Mars product Balisto, a 'healthy chocolate bar'. The 1980s was the first period of the 'green wave'. Everything had to be environmentally friendly (saving power, reduced effluent, etc.) and healthy. Balisto fitted this trend exactly: it is a product with healthy and natural ingredients and covered with chocolate. Correspondingly, the communication suggested 'something healthy from nature'. The TV commercial showed a farmer with a horse and cart loaded with wheat. The endlines were 'nature that tastes crispy' and 'naturally different'. But after some time the company noticed that it reached only a limited target group with the chosen positioning and, consequently, it had limited the success of the product and the brand.

So, for that reason, Mars looked for a new positioning and arrived at a very simple solution by posing the seemingly obvious question: Why do people buy chocolate bars in the first place? What are the drivers? With the answer to this question, the company quickly found the category driver goal of chocolate: enjoyment from good taste. The communication was changed from 'healthy and natural with chocolate' to 'chocolate with healthy, natural ingredients'. Mars had understood that people weren't buying chocolate to receive healthy nutrition; they bought chocolate as enjoyment. That is the basic goal that is meant to be satisfied by chocolate – for that reason it was key to service this as a priority.

The trend was to eat chocolate for enjoyment but which was healthy at the same time. The new positioning primarily served the goal of enjoyment but importantly supplemented the healthy aspect. Sales rocketed and made Balisto the market leader in the chocolate bar segment of the German market a few years later. Chocolate first has to be chocolate and to taste good before it can serve any additional goal. However, very often focusing solely on the explicit goals does not leave enough room for differentiation. Whiter than white? Cleaner than clean? If it's hard to convey perceivable differentiation of the level to which the explicit goals can be achieved, then the implicit level not only boosts relevance (by achieving implicit goals), it also offers the potential to differentiate our brands and products in a relevant way.

Therefore, in order to provide the best possible value proposition – relevant and differentiating – for our customers, we have to intertwine explicit goals and implicit goals. To see how this can be done let's imagine we need to develop a proposition for a new car braking system. Its key benefit is that, when appropriate, it alerts the driver and stops the car. The explicit goal that this fulfils is obvious: preventing an accident by getting the car to stop more quickly. Now to what implicit goal could this be potentially linked in order to increase goal value? Safety is an obvious candidate – we want to protect ourselves and our family by preventing accidents. The excitement territory can also be linked to this feature and the explicit goal – we can drive faster and enjoy driving more dynamically because the system enables us to react more quickly. Autonomy can be linked to this as well because owning this advanced technology product provides superiority. The resulting value propositions intertwine the explicit-functional goals with the implicit-psychological goals (see Figure 5.9).

But now we have developed three potential value propositions. How do we choose the right one? At this point the brand comes into play. In order to be credible, the value proposition needs to fit the brand. For Volvo the safety proposition would be credible. The following TV ad links the

	Signal	⇄	Explicit goal	⇄	Implicit goal
Mercedes	Automatic braking system	→ ←	Shorter braking distance	→ ←	Superiority
BMW	Automatic braking system	→ ←	Shorter braking distance	→ ←	Driving pleasure
Volvo	Automatic braking system	→ ←	Shorter braking distance	→ ←	Safety

Figure 5.9 Value-based proposition: intertwining product feature with explicit and implicit goals

product with the safety goal. We see a laboratory with the Volvo on a test track. The customers sit in the back seats where children would normally sit (an effective signal for safety). The engineer, in the driving seat, explains what they are going to do now: they will drive straight at another car and then their car will stop itself automatically. The customers look a bit scared and link hands tightly. The demonstration starts, the car stops itself because of the braking system, and the customers are shown to be visibly relieved and feeling secure.

For Mercedes, in contrast, the superiority proposition would be the route to go, and this was nicely translated in the 'Old Father Time' TV ad. A man drives through the woods. Suddenly the Grim Reaper sits beside him. The man stares at him. The Grim Reaper starts laughing and says, 'Sorry.' At that moment the braking system starts to brake, making the car stop just in front of a truck blocking the road. After some seconds of looking shocked the driver turns to the Grim Reaper and says, 'Sorry.' The braking system metaphorically provided superiority over death.

Mercedes produced a follow-up advert. A man drives through the woods and suddenly sees a deer standing in the middle of the road. Thanks to the braking system he is able to stop. As a result, the deer and other woodland animals start to dance like John Travolta singing the Bee Gees' song 'Staying Alive'.

This ad clearly dramatizes the explicit goal. However, it lacks the implicit level. It is not staged in such a way that the braking system and, hence, the resultant shorter braking distance are instrumental in achieving an implicit goal. One could argue that the ad is entertaining and that entertainment is a goal for people as well. Certainly being entertained is a potential goal. This is why we watch TV: we want to be entertained. However, the perceived goal value is based on associations between the product, the brand and consumer goals. Therefore, if the goal associated

Propositions provide the highest value for the consumer when they intertwine the explicit with the implicit goals.

with the brand is to be entertained, the brain would learn a connection between the braking system and entertainment. This is hardly relevant in this case. Viewed from this perspective, it comes as no surprise that the follow-up ad was taken off air after just two weeks.

What we have learned in this chapter

- Goal-based valuation is the most sophisticated level of value in the human brain, and it is a key concept in our journey to answer the question of why we buy what we buy.
- Brands and products are a means to an end and this instrumentality in achieving goals is their true motivational power.
- The instrumentality of brands in helping to achieve goals is based on learned associations between brands and goals. These associations trigger expectations which determine the expected goal value of a brand. Purchase decisions are based on this goal value.
- There are two levels of goal value: explicit and implicit. In order to maximize goal value, brands need to be linked to both the explicit and the implicit level. Propositions provide the highest value for the consumer when they intertwine the explicit with the implicit goals.

What this means to us as marketers

- For a strategy – from defining the market, positioning, R&D to segmentation – to have a strong impact on sales, it should be derived from relevant consumer goals. Identifying and understanding the relevant goals in a market enables us to evaluate the potential of a positioning: for how many consumers is a particular goal the dominant purchase driver for our category?
- The basis for relevance is to serve the dominant, explicit goals in the market at least as well as the competition does. Strong associations with the explicit goals grant the right to play in a category. Rule of thumb: the brand which owns the dominant explicit goal in the category is the market leader.
- If there is no superiority possible on explicit goals, the implicit goal level provides the lever for differentiation. In doing so, the specific implicit goals chosen must boost relevance and ensure relevant differentiation.
- A value proposition consists of a link between explicit and implicit goals (e.g. an automatic braking system stops the car more quickly *so that* the driver feels superior). The connection between explicit and implicit goals is not arbitrary: the entire product experience determines which implicit goals can be credibly linked to the explicit goal.

6

From Positioning to Touchpoints

Bringing Value to Life

So far we have seen many facets of the implicit level of marketing, ranging from perception to motivated behaviour. In this chapter we will focus on how we can efficiently and effectively implement our goal-based strategy to create product experiences and communication. We will also explore how to judge whether an execution credibly fits this strategy.

Closing the implementation gap

When we summarize what we have learned in the previous chapter, marketing appears, on the face of it, to be quite simple: we have to create a value proposition consisting of both explicit and implicit goals, link the implicit to the explicit goals, translate this proposition into signals which will activate mental concepts within the consumer, and then, if these mental concepts fit with the consumer's active goal better than those activated by competitors, they will buy our brand or product (see Figure 6.1).

There are two main barriers to more successful marketing: first, the strategy is not based on consumer goals, and second, the signals used to convey the value proposition do not activate the intended mental concepts and goals in the consumer's mind.

That appears to be fairly straightforward, but we all know how challenging it is to develop a compelling strategy and to implement it across all touchpoints. It can take months, dozens of meetings and hundreds of hours to discuss the strategy alone. When it comes to implementing the strategy, the discussions become increasingly intense. Which creative idea will work best? How do we optimally convey the core benefits? Which music or testimonial should we choose? The question of which signal best implements the strategy is frequently a matter of heated and lengthy discussions and debates. Often the situation gets even worse once we receive feedback from market research. Some elements work well, others do not. One route works well in one country but fails in another.

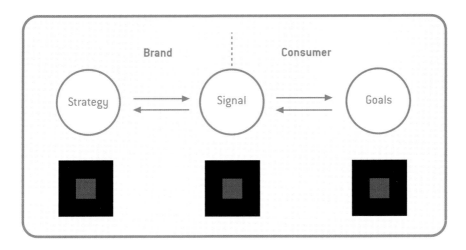

Figure 6.1 Implementation: translating strategy into signals that address consumer goals

So, where exactly does the challenge lie in implementing our strategies? What makes this such a difficult task? Where are the traps and how can we prevent them? Let's see how the explicit and implicit levels of decision making, and what we have learned so far, can help here.

We start by looking again at the relaunch of the Tropicana pack design, which led to a loss of €30 million in just two months, as it illustrates some of the more typical pitfalls. Starting with the category of 'orange juice', the explicit goal is to get a fresh and tasty drink. This is what the original packaging perfectly addresses: what could be more tasty and fresh than drinking the juice straight from the fruit? It is a juice directly derived from a fruit which is intuitively associated with health benefits. This is especially relevant given the occasion when orange juice is prototypically consumed: in the morning. The explicit goal of drinking something in the morning can be achieved with any drink but, compared with possible substitutes such as water or soft drinks, orange juice is both fresher and perceived to be more healthy.

So what implicit goal does a parent achieve by giving orange juice to the family? This product is linked to the implicit goal territory of 'security' – taking care of the family, doing something good for them, protecting them by giving them vitamins. At the same time this goal is met in a simple and pragmatic way, because it can be achieved quickly and with low behavioural costs (compared with cutting up oranges and squeezing them oneself). The goal-based value proposition for orange juice might be captured thus: 'the simple way to take care of the family (implicit goal) by giving them tasty, fresh orange juice (explicit goal).' If we now look at the new pack design it becomes obvious that it reduces the fit with these goals because its signals are fundamentally different. The glass no longer signals freshness; therefore this explicit goal is achieved to a much lesser extent. Because the design is clean, more minimal and fits the convention of 'cool, modern design', it serves the design prototype of premium brands which in turn stands for exclusivity. However, on an implicit level, exclusivity is a code for distance and separation, which is the opposite of the security goal territory. Figure 6.2 shows that the design change positioned the brand in a very different, much less relevant (given the category and brand) goal territory.

It would be a mistake, of course, to attribute such failure just to the specific brand and the people involved because similar mistakes happen every day across many companies. So what can we learn from this case? Peter Arnell, the designer responsible for the new design, says the objective of the redesign was to 'rejuvenate, reengineer, rethink, reparticipate in popular culture' and to 'emotionally connect with consumers'. This illustrates a key barrier to efficient implementation: our strategy papers, and especially our briefing documents, often consist of *our* (internal) objectives that we want to achieve instead of focusing on the consumer and their explicit and implicit goals.

Another major barrier is that the objective of emotionally connecting with consumers is very vague and offers a lot of room for subjective interpretation.

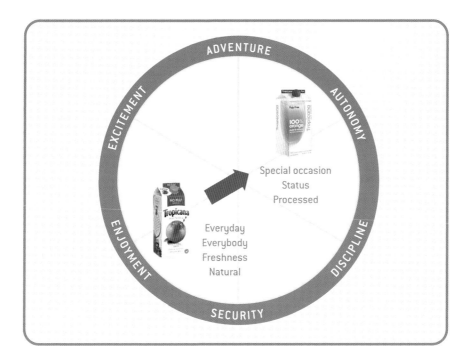

Figure 6.2 The new packaging of Tropicana addresses very different consumer goals

Why 'emotion' does not help

We have all used and heard the objective that we need 'to emotionally connect with consumers', that we need to bond with them, and that we need to 'emotionalize' our brands and products. The term 'emotion' is a very important concept in marketing, so let's take a closer look at it. It's actually one of the big obstacles to efficient marketing, especially when implementing strategies across touchpoints.

First of all, what are emotions about? In marketing we are not so much interested in the neuronal or psychophysiological aspects but we focus instead on the emotional benefits that drive purchase decisions. This is, among other things, inspired by consumer response in market research:

207

consumers often refer to well-being or feeling good when they try to explain why they buy what they buy. Therefore feeling good, feeling well and positive emotions seem to be plausible drivers of purchase behaviour. But what does science have to say about the role of emotions in motivated behaviour? In the words of renowned psychologists Charles S. Carver and Michael F. Scheier in the *Oxford Handbook of Human Action*: 'Affect can be positive, neutral or negative for any goal-directed action, depending on how well or poorly the action seems to be attaining the goal.' In other words, emotions give feedback on goal achievement.

Let's say we want to win a tennis match (performance goal) and when we lose a few games, this triggers anger or frustration. These emotions are feedback signals informing us where we are at regarding our goal of winning. Goal achievement is what triggers 'well-being' and 'feeling good', and because consumers have limited access to their implicit goals, they talk about the outcome of their decision when they are asked about the reasons for their purchases, rather than the true underlying, motivational force. The positive affect results out of goal achievement. We experience well-being no matter if we drive a Porsche, eat some tasty chocolate or remove a stain from our favourite shirt. It is the only conscious experience we have of the implicit valuation processes within the autopilot.

If we look at current advertising campaigns it appears that often the positive affect of watching an ad is taken as one key objective of communication. As long as it's funny and entertaining, people will like the ad and this in turn will help persuasion. This leads to briefings where we ask agencies to come up with break-through, entertaining and engaging advertisements. Positive emotions triggered while watching an advert are, of course, nothing bad – the enjoyment will be part of the brand's associative network – but no customer buys the product merely because the campaign was entertaining. There are hardly any brands that convey negative emotions, so how could we differentiate based on positive emotions? By being even funnier or more entertaining than our competitors?

Setting aside scientific hair-splitting, the term emotion has severe practical issues. There is often a discussion about what is more important: the price and the product benefit *or* the emotional benefit. Do we want to invest in an image campaign *or* a hard selling campaign? Is it brand *or* product that drives the purchase decision? Underlying these discussions is the basic assumption that the 'hard' facts (price, product features, etc.) are 'rational' while the 'soft' elements (brand, image) are more 'emotional'. Product and brand are treated as trade-offs because we think of them using the emotional *versus* rational model of decision making.

Why do we have so many discussions though? Why do we argue about just how emotional or rational an advert ought to be? Because both these aspects result in totally different signals. A 'rational' TV ad looks completely different from an 'emotional' one. An emotional newspaper ad or pack design differs completely from a rational, informative ad or design. We are not arguing about whether both emotional and rational benefits are important; what we do discuss in marketing, often controversially, however, is which of these two aspects is more important and is the customer's priority. In the end, this often boils down to what we personally believe: one person might believe in the power of emotions, someone else in the power of factual, 'rational' information to persuade. The only problem with all this is that we must, at some point, come to a decision.

What happens as a result of this is that the connection between these two levels becomes lost. The emotional versus rational model often results in compromises and prolonged discussions about how many seconds the product needs to be shown in a TV commercial. Why exactly is it so difficult to bring 'emotional' and 'rational' aspects together? Why do we struggle so much with this? A short look at where this thinking originates can help us to understand this challenge better. The idea that emotion and

Figure 6.3 Which design conveys 'light biscuit' better?

reason are opponents refers back to the Greek philosopher Plato, who talked about emotion being the black horse that needs to be controlled by the white horse which symbolizes reason and rationality. This dualism made its way through history, including Descartes and Kant. Today this thinking manifests itself in our briefings: we tend to have one section for the emotional benefit and one for the functional benefit. More often than not, the two are not connected or intertwined.

The concept of emotions is too vague to guide implementation. Emotions are also too generic to enable relevant differentiation in a market.

The notion of goals, however, does not entertain this dualism. If we think of products as serving explicit goals, and of brands as serving implicit goals, then there is no problem in creating a value proposition that weaves together the explicit and the implicit goal levels.

Goals guide implementation because they are linked to signals

If the goal is to communicate 'a light biscuit', which of the two pack designs in Figure 6.3 is more suitable?

What has our brain learned in relation to 'light things'? Where do light things go? The spontaneous answer is 'they float upwards'. Obviously, gravity makes even light things actually fall downwards; however, we've learned through our everyday experiences that heavy things push or pull us down, for example when we are carrying a heavy bag – and light is the opposite of heavy. The brain learns through countless situations in which 'light' and 'top' appear together that these two signals are coupled. So in our associative memory there is a link between 'light' and 'top'. Put differently, 'top' turns into a code for 'light'. In marketing we can 'borrow' this memory when signalling the lightness of the biscuits integral to a consumer goal of healthiness or dieting. So it's not surprising that, according to a study by researchers at Ohio State University, most of those questioned considered the design in which the biscuits are displayed at the bottom of the pack as heavier. Does that, consequently, mean that the other packaging is 'better'? The answer of whether it's right or wrong depends on the goal that customers want to achieve with the product. For products for which 'heaviness' might be seen as a positive attribute (e.g. chocolate biscuits), people who were questioned preferred designs in which the product was displayed at the bottom. With 'light' diet products, however, packaging with the product displayed nearer the top was preferred. It seems that this is not about what looks nicer and is more pleasing to the customer's eye but specifically about the goal that consumers are hoping to achieve with a product.

This example illustrates another practical benefit of working with goals: they are directly linked to signals and thus help in implementing brand strategies, as long as these strategies are conceived in terms of consumer goals. To better understand this let's once again look at emotions. One of the leading scientists in the field of emotion is Paul Ekman. His research shows that there are six basic emotions that can be expressed and understood around the world: anger, disgust, fear, happiness, sadness and surprise. By looking at this list it becomes evident that there are only two positive emotions: joy and surprise. As a result, briefing agencies to 'emotionalize the brand' often results in adverts that show happy people – no matter whether it is a bank, a retailer, a car or anything else. Alternatively the focus is on the entertaining character of the TV ad in order to make the consumer experience enjoyable when watching it.

Briefing 'emotions' opens the door to intense debates. Is the new Tropicana packaging emotional? Why? Why not? How should a woman look if she experiences an emotional benefit? Hard to tell, isn't it? The term 'emotion' is much too vague to effectively guide implementation, whereas goals are very precise. Since our brain uses goals as filters to detect which products fit with them, our associative network already contains many associations between goals and signals. In order to achieve goals and monitor goal achievement on autopilot, we need to know what to look for, therefore we learn which signals are linked to particular goals.

By positioning our brands and products using goals, we have clear guidelines for implementation because of the signals that are linked to the brand goal in the associative memory of consumers (see Figure 6.4).

Product signals such as colour, shape and size tell consumers which goal they can achieve with them and, for active goals, they implicitly look out

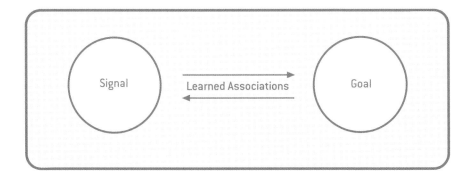

Figure 6.4 Signals and goals are connected by learned associations

for signals which are coupled to the achievement of those particular goals. We saw the eye-tracking example where people in a hungry state focused on the McDonald's logo. More generally, we see what we want. Looking for a can of Coke enhances the processing of red areas in our visual input by increasing the neuronal sensitivity for that particular colour. In other words, goals are directly and immediately coupled to signals. This is enormously helpful for our marketing practice because clear guidelines for the selection of signals, e.g. in communication, then follow.

So, the term 'emotion' distracts from the real drivers of purchase – it opens up a trade-off metaphor, it is hardly a help in guiding our strategy and it doesn't enable us, systematically, to manage our brand across its touchpoints. But the 'emotional versus rational' model is so deeply ingrained in us that it seems unrealistic, really, to replace it any time soon. So if we do continue to use the word 'emotion', and hence the dualistic model of brand versus product, we should make sure that we think of emotional benefits as goals.

Employing a goal-based strategy not only ensures relevance, it also offers clear guidance for translating the strategy into signals. The reason for this is that there are learned associations in the brain between signals and goals.

People buy categories first

One major challenge in devising and implementing brand strategies is differentiation from competition. We know that differentiation is key for a brand strategy to be successful. It is usually reasonable to assume that we cannot differentiate our products and brands on the explicit goal level, and hence we need to seek differentiation elsewhere as a priority. The danger that lies in this approach is the possibility of forgetting the explicit goal altogether and hence risking a lack of relevance. We saw this with Balisto, the healthy chocolate bar, in the previous chapter. People buy categories first and foremost, which is indicated by their shopping lists – consumers rarely write down the brand.

Most of the times they note the category: they write coffee, soup or margarine, rather than Nescafé, Heinz or Flora.

Serving the elementary explicit goals is therefore vital. Interestingly, the brand that owns the explicit goal is market leader. In our own work we have seen this principle working in all the categories we have analyzed, be it detergents, cosmetics or telecommunications. As a consequence, in non-mature markets it is key to focus on the explicit goal and try to own it. Being number two in the market and increasing the brand's association with the explicit goals to the level of the market leader helps to increase penetration.

Suggestion

To identify the explicit basic goals of your category, try answering the following question: 'If there was only one brand in this category, then what goal must it fulfil? If the product or service did not exist, what would people do or buy instead?'

When implementing campaigns which address basic goals, we need to identify appropriate signals. A good example is the advert from Lenor shown in Figure 6.5. We see a family getting dressed in the morning. These scenes establish the topic of softness which is the core goal of the softener category. The product demo shows two towels with a peach rubbed on each one. On the towel that had been washed with Lenor the peach's skin isn't damaged.

Some may argue that this is not realistic because no woman would ever rub a peach on a towel. One could also argue that it is not terribly creative or entertaining and that consumers would not be inclined to look at

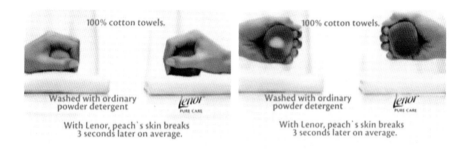

Figure 6.5 The Lenor advert establishes an association between the brand and the explicit goal of the softener category

it a second or third time. However, the advert was very successful. From the brain's perspective, the communication does what it is supposed to be doing and does it effectively and efficiently: it establishes a link between the product and the explicit goal of the category, softness. And this is exactly what we should do if our ambition is to develop effective communication: use existing connections between signals and goals rather than trying to establish new ones. The existing connections have already been validated thousands of times and this provides a strength that even heavyweight media expenditure cannot match.

The signals in the Lenor advert convey the softness proposition and, in so doing, strengthen the association between the brand and the goal. This uses an existing association because we already know that a peach's skin is sensitive and fragile. Hence the concept of softness is triggered and linked with the brand. Using the peach as a symbol for sensitive skin is creative because it has never been used before in the category. It is creative and yet it exploits existing associative links between the skin of a peach and softness.

Fortunately our brain is flexible so that we can communicate concepts not only in a straightforward way, as in the Lenor ad, but also on a more metaphorical level. The 'Surfer' TV ad for the Guinness brand is a nice example of this. The ad uses the metaphor of surfers waiting for the ultimate wave to represent the anticipation of the perfect pint. As they surf, galloping horses metamorphose from the waves.

The TV ad dramatizes the unique aspect of the product experience – the length of time it takes to be poured on draught and the strength of the beer. When it is poured, it initially produces a lot of foam. This is the reason for the delay, needing time to let it settle before we can drink it. This product attribute was dramatized metaphorically through the campaign concept of 'Good things come to those who wait'. And this idea, which – even if metaphorically – is very closely linked to the product experience, was successfully implemented by Guinness in a number of adverts. If we were to show this in a focus group, we might hear reactions like 'this is not credible', 'what does this have to do with beer?', 'I cannot identify with the surfer' or 'the horses are not realistic'. Indeed, a market research agency suggested leaving the horses out as consumers regarded them as unrealistic. If we look at it from a more implicit perspective, such comments are hardly relevant. The horses and the way they are portrayed signal that the waves are strong and wild. This is without doubt associated with the concepts of strength and power. And this fits with why people drink Guinness.

We can be very creative in our executions as long as we use established associations between signals and goals.

Guidance beyond formalism

Because translating our strategy into execution involves so many discussions and insecurities, we are often attracted to the idea of ensuring consistency and judging right from wrong by guiding execution through the means of style guides, key visuals and formalistic checklists of signals. However, we learned that our brain is more flexible than this when we looked at the Halle Berry study in Chapter 3. It is not important to the brain how the Halle Berry brand is encoded, whether as an image or merely as text – as long as the *meaning* of 'Halle Berry' is recognizable, the neurons fire. In the brain, therefore, there are neurons which decode the brand – in this case Halle Berry – according to similarity in content, no matter how this content is packaged. Let's now look in more detail at how to manage consistency and how to prevent the traps that go along with formalistic approaches.

Du darfst is a Unilever brand from Germany and the name translates as 'you may' or 'you're allowed to'. Originally, the brand launched as a low-fat spread but is now an umbrella brand for a range of low-calorie food products. Let's start with an advert from the 1990s (see Figure 6.6), which successfully launched the brand.

Let's apply the key questions that our brain answers while processing these signals: what is it and what does it stand for? We can see a woman in her early 30s in a red dress walking outside. She carries a document folder, indicating that she is going to work. She smiles and walks in an agile way. She passes the window of a restaurant and, by chance, she catches a reflection of herself, appreciates what she sees and continues on her way. What goals does this storyline signal? Wearing a close-fitting red dress in public

Figure 6.6 The advert that was the birth mark of the *Du darfst* brand

is promotional and the goal territory signalled is autonomy since such behaviour requires confidence. Her glance in the mirrored window happens by accident, implying that she is not checking herself out (which would be prevention oriented). She is pleased with what she sees and this is linked to the implicit goal of being proud of oneself. Interestingly, she is on her own, with no one else around, which means that her confidence is based on her own judgement and is independent from others. This again serves the autonomy territory. The agile way she walks pays into vitality, which is further supported by the uplifting music.

After launch, competition became intense as more and more 'light' ranges and products were launched, so the brand started to change its communication. Subsequent campaigns were not successful so, as market share declined, the brand brought the red dress back into its advertising (see Figure 6.7).

At first glance it would appear that this new advert should work well, too. An attractive woman goes to work and wears a red dress. She sees herself accidentally in the mirror and likes what she sees. The voice-over claims

Figure 6.7 Despite formal similarities, this advert addresses different goals

'fall in love with yourself again', which supports this message. However, despite the similarities at an explicit level, the overall implicit message is very different from the original ad. First of all, the woman is different. She is younger and the way she wears her hair indicates both her age and that she is not as senior and elegant as the woman in the previous ad. The dress is different as well: it is sleeveless, low-cut and has a slit hem. The style and cut are not as classical. She's carrying a handbag rather than something work-related. Interpreting all of this together, as the autopilot does with its 11 million bits, the red dress in this execution doesn't stand for confidence. It's also noticeable that the scene in which she looks at herself in the mirror doesn't take place in public this time but when she's alone, in the enclosed space of a lift. This also works against the intended goal of confidence. Before she exits the lift she checks her hair again to make sure she looks okay. This seems natural and works sympathetically, but these aspects are not helpful in relation to conveying the desired goal: her behaviour doesn't fit the goal of confidence. She then receives a compliment from the male receptionist, which seemingly makes her happy. However, recognition from a third party undermines the possibility of her autonomy and independence. Moreover, is a compliment from someone like a receptionist really likely to please a self-assured woman?

What this case study shows is that, while much was similar at a formal level (e.g. 'advertising mandatories' such as the red dress), as well as the same explicit goals being addressed (low-calorie food), the two TVCs clearly addressed different implicit goals. Had a goal-based proposition been used, one that intertwined explicit and implicit goals by saying 'show that with *Du darfst* you are confident, independent and proud of what you see', then the second ad – which was taken off air after a short time – would never have been made.

Using a goal-based proposition not only ensures relevance, it also enables precise steering of the implementation.

Another case showing how implicit goals can help to ensure consistency within, and across, campaigns is Cadbury. At the beginning of this book we talked about the 'Gorilla' advert and how the client did not consider the sequels (see Figure 6.8) to be successful and they were taken off air quickly.

Now let's look at the 'Gorilla' ad first. The soundtrack, 'In the air tonight', creates a context which is calm/gentle and the setting, indoors, is proto-typically female territory. Next we see a close-up of a gorilla. This is incongruous in the context of chocolate and the music. The gorilla is a dangerous and powerful beast. Its eyes close and its nostrils flare, indicat-ing that it appears to be listening to the music, and so it is no immediate threat. It seems to be enjoying the music. While the music builds towards its well-known drum break, the gorilla flexes its neck and shoulders, showing that it is loosening up in anticipation of something. The gorilla is on its own, which, together with these actions, indicates individuality and a 'me moment'. The soundtrack builds to its climax and the gorilla is revealed to be sitting at a drum kit and it joins in with the drumming in an explosive and inspired, human-like way. The gorilla throws back its head several times as if in ecstasy. This imagery and activity are perceived as bizarre, intriguing and amusing. The music fades and the gorilla is replaced by a pack shot of Cadbury Dairy Milk with the super 'A glass and a half full of joy'.

Spurred on by the hype and discussion caused by 'Gorilla', Cadbury briefed for a follow-up advert called 'Trucks'. The brief to 'rediscover the joy' was identical to the one that produced the 'Gorilla' ad. 'Trucks' opens with an image of an aeroplane taking off from a runway. It is outdoors and night-time, which are codes for male territory. Queen's 'Don't stop me now' soundtrack starts over images of various airport trucks being started up and prepared for something. Images of exhaust pipes and racing driver uniforms again signal masculine codes. The trucks line up on the runway and start to race (autonomy). There is fast camera action and cuts to show the speed and manoeuvring of the trucks, some of which is remi-niscent of chase scenes in action movies (adventure). Each truck has a way

Figure 6.8 The Cadbury 'Gorilla' ad and its sequel, 'Trucks'

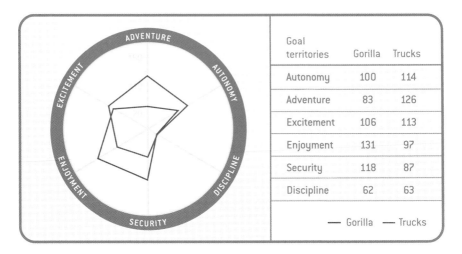

Goal territories	Gorilla	Trucks
Autonomy	100	114
Adventure	83	126
Excitement	106	113
Enjoyment	131	97
Security	118	87
Discipline	62	63

—— Gorilla —— Trucks

Figure 6.9 Research confirms different goal profiles for the two ads

of getting in front and/or of stopping the others from overtaking it. What can we learn from mapping these adverts onto the decode goal map™?

Figure 6.9 clearly shows that the associations triggered by the two adverts are very different. The two adverts address different goal territories. 'Trucks' activates goals such as masculinity, competition and aggression, resulting in higher scores on autonomy and adventure. 'Gorilla' triggers enjoyment and security more strongly than 'Trucks'. How can this be given that the brief was identical? 'Rediscover the joy' is not precise enough in terms of desired goals. It does not guide implementation because the word 'joy' is open to many interpretations. Both adverts fit with 'joy', but they convey different connotations of joy. Using the implicit goal map we can not only measure the associations of adverts very precisely but distinguish between different connotations of joy such as the joy of discovery, fun or adventure and the joy of competition.

How do we know which implicit profile is right for the brand (see Figure 6.10)? Let's first look at the category: milk chocolate in block format. It

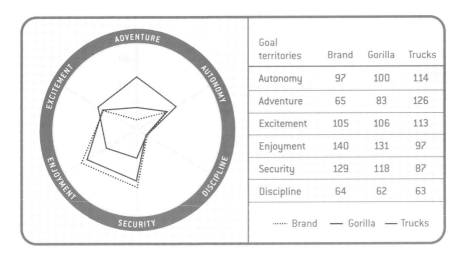

Figure 6.10 Comparing the brand profile with the adverts

is characterized by a high milk-fat content, which makes it creamy and implies melting in the mouth. If we consider when and why we consume milk chocolate, it is not surprising to find that it has its core in the enjoyment and security territories. Chocolate is often referred to as comfort food after all. In a study we measured the implicit brand profile of Cadbury Dairy Milk. One result was that Cadbury owns the basic goals of milk chocolate, with the key implicit associations being tradition, trust, warmth, relaxation, enjoyment and sociability. Cadbury Dairy Milk delivers the core block chocolate rewards, which is why it is No 1 in the UK market. Comparing the brand profile with the two adverts reveals that 'Gorilla' has a higher overlap than 'Trucks'. Since the brief was 'Rediscover the joy', which does not imply a brand repositioning, a creative advert that fits the brand was what was required. If the brand had wanted to move into adventure and autonomy territories, the 'Trucks' advert would have been more appropriate. Using the implicit goals as a reference to sharpen the territory we want to head towards can help to ensure consistency at a proposition level and, at the

The implicit goal level adds significant guidance for deciding which execution serves the strategy best.

same time, it enables flexibility at the signal level, and hence maintains endless scope for creativity.

360 degree – how to avoid goal dilution

The task of marketing is obviously more complex than simply ensuring consistent TV ads. The whole marketing mix needs to be orchestrated. Multi-product brands face the challenge of positioning each SKU distinctively under one umbrella brand. How can the perspective of goals help here? Let's look at the Müller brand and how they aligned communication and packaging (see Figure 6.11).

The TV ad, shown in 2011, clearly addresses the goal territory of excitement – it shows how the yoghurt turns a dangerous, unpleasant, negative world into a place of fun. The world becomes a playground again by taking away all the pressure and seriousness. This meaning is also 'baked in' to the product. Looking from above, it looks square and has two sections. Because the extra ingredients in the 'corner' are meant to complement and not dominate, there is one big section for the yoghurt and one small chamber for the extras. The sections divide the square into two, but not symmetrically. On opening, the lid is pulled off and the content of both chambers becomes visible. We tend to eat this yoghurt by

Figure 6.11 A TV advert for Müller, and its packaging

first pouring the contents of the little chamber into the bigger one. This solid square shape is broken by folding over the corner. Crack! When we fold over the chamber, we hear a breaking sound. We are left with a separate triangular section and an adjoined asymmetrical shape. A regular shape is turned into an unstable shape. In the figurative sense we break through stability and this signals the goal territory of excitement.

Overall this experience fits with the proposition conveyed in the 2011 TV ad. However, the 2D design of the packaging doesn't at all. The brand relaunched in 2011 with both new packaging and advertising. The packaging seems to have been designed to a brief to 'own' the category in-store via the use of a strong block of (blue) colour on its tubs and merchandizing trays. This implicitly signals that the brand is mainstream, for everyone, and successful and dominant in the yoghurt category. However, this is the internal sales objective, and doesn't help to signal the consumer's goals. The 2D design conveys simplicity, it is plain and serious. The design is associated with the goal territory of discipline and this is the exact opposite of fun, which is all about breaking out of the rules and the seriousness.

Now, one could argue that overall goal value is increased because the advert and the packaging cover two distinct goal territories rather than one. This is a fair point, so what insights does science provide to test this hypothesis? The key insight is called 'goal dilution'. One could argue that the value of a brand or a product is highest if it is positioned on several, unrelated goals that consumers might want to achieve. However, the model of goal dilution shows that, actually, the opposite is true.

According to psychologists Zhang, Fishbach and Kruglanski, the strength of an association between a brand and a goal depends on the goal being unique. In other words, if a brand is linked to several goals, each of these connections will be weakened. Google stands for the goal to search, while Yahoo is linked with being a portal plus a search engine. People consider

Google to be the better search engine because the search goal is diluted due to the additional goals Yahoo tries to serve. We should therefore focus on a single-minded goal value proposition because that's the only chance we have to be seen as being the best in this respect. When we manage only one product, this is hard enough to adhere to because we always fear that we might lose something if we do not include a whole list of benefits in our proposition. Concept test results certainly support this approach because the more benefits the concept contains, the better the test results. However, since distinct goals need distinct signals, such an approach would lead to ineffective implementation.

That's when we're managing only one brand, so what do we do when we have an umbrella brand to manage? In the case of multi-product brands, the insight of goal dilution implies that, in order to keep the goal value of the umbrella brand and the individual SKUs at a maximum level, we have to use goals that are distinctive, but strongly associated. They need to be distinctive in order to provide marginal utility in the portfolio. If an SKU does not address a distinct goal, its impact on sales will come only from greater overall shelf presence.

Coca-Cola's campaign 'Group Hug' is a good example of how the same goal can be applied consistently across touchpoints (see Figure 6.12). This can help to guide media planning and even provide springboards for other touchpoints. The Coke brand is strongly associated with the security territory. Therefore the implementation of 'Group Hug' fits this territory perfectly (source: http://www.forbes.com/sites/anthonykosner/2012/04/11/hug-me-coca-cola-introduces-gesture-based-marketing-in-singapore/).

The figure shows that the campaign was heavily based on outdoor ads. Therefore the signals not only fit with the goal of security but contact with the campaign occurs in a situation when this goal is active – when

Figure 6.12 Consistent implementation of a security goal across touchpoints

we are out and about and find ourselves standing in a crowd of strangers. We have no connection to them and therefore we feel isolated even though so many people are standing beside us. The image in the top right shows how outdoor media were deployed to capitalize on this insight. The idea of hugging was taken even further by creating vending machines that would dispense the bottle only if the machine was hugged. Working with goals ensures that we can use the currency that is relevant for the consumer – the main benefit lies with more precise guidance of

Implicit goals can effectively guide implementation across touchpoints, countries and product ranges because they are universal and fundamental motivational drivers that transcend specific touchpoints, products or brands.

implementation. In so doing it enables marketers to steer execution and to be better able to judge right from wrong.

Borrowed memory – the source of objectivity

So goals can help to guide implementation by adding more precision. However, even with the most profound strategic basis, marketing still faces an issue: how can we judge whether a signal conveys the proposition that we intend it to communicate? When agencies present proposals – be it storyboards, treatments, outdoor campaigns or social media – there is often a lot of subjective guessing, opinions, tastes and beliefs involved in evaluating the proposals, leading to controversial discussions and, even worse, to compromises that often do not exploit the full potential of the proposal. What is missing is an objective approach for judging whether this signal is right or wrong given the intended value proposition.

Most of the time we delegate this discussion to the consumer by pre-testing the advertisement or packaging. But if it fails the test, it is often unclear why, and, more importantly, how to fix it. One often hears recommendations from research agencies such as 'make it more distinctive/memorable/emotional/etc.', yet this type of focus on requirements still begs the question of *how* to do it. What exactly would make the advert more distinctive or memorable? Overall, this situation stops marketing teams and agencies from learning and thereby improving, since learning requires precise feedback and guidance. Of course, there are many cases where successful products and campaigns have been produced, but more often than not they are based on the intuition of the experts involved. Intuition is great but hard to make explicit and therefore hard to share with others, and hard to justify when challenged. Intuition depends on the specific individual in the process which is a barrier for consistency over time (due to change in personnel) as well as across countries and operating units.

So how can we be more objective about agency propositions and signals in general? The brain translates signals into mental concepts, which we summarized with the 'X = Y' formula. One could argue that everyone has their own equation, and that the translation of signals into concepts, and therefore how well they address the relevant goal, is purely subjective, based on individual tastes and preferences. The good news is that this is not the case. The translation is rule-based and far from arbitrary or subjective in nature.

Research by psychologist Samuel Gosling illustrates this fact in a fascinating way. He showed respondents pictures of the apartments of students who were unknown to them, and they were asked to judge the apartment owner's personality by filling out a standardized and validated inventory from psychological science that captures the main aspects of personality (see Figure 6.13). The results were compared with the personality profiles that the owners themselves had completed, as well as with profiles completed by the owners' friends. The result was astonishing. The strangers were able to accurately decode the owner's personality just from the picture of the apartment, and were even more accurate than the owner's friends' ratings for three out of five dimensions in the test. They were unable to express exactly which element or signal in the picture had formed their image of the owner, but they were nevertheless able to decode the pattern.

This fascinating result illustrates that we share a deep, mostly implicit, understanding of what signals stand for. If the meaning of signals was arbitrary and subjective, this result could not happen. Not only that, but we would be unable to communicate effectively either. If one holds the door for a colleague, we just know that this stands for friendliness and for being kind. We even have a shared understanding not only of gestures, symbols or words but of signals that we haven't ever seen before. Looking at Figure 6.14, which shape is the 'buba' and which is the 'kiki'?

Describe
the resident!

Figure 6.13 Strangers are able to accurately decode the personality of the resident based on photographs of the apartment

Reproduced by permission of Sam Gosling. Sourced from his book *Snoop: What Your Stuff Says About You*

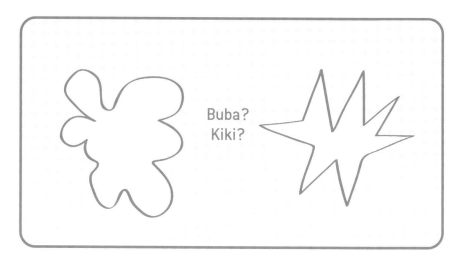

Buba?
Kiki?

Figure 6.14 Which of the two shapes is the 'buba' and which is the 'kiki'?

None of us has seen these particular shapes before, nor have we heard these words (since they do not exist). But hardly anyone guesses that the round, soft shape is the kiki. The reason is that the letter 'k', and the staccato sound of the word, are similar to the 'jagged' and 'cutting' shape on the right, whereas the letters 'b' and 'u', and the sound of the word, are more of a match for the soft, bulbous form on the left. As such, almost without exception, people link 'buba' to the shape on the left and 'kiki' to the shape on the right. Did you do the same? Is that your subjective opinion or is it arbitrary? Neither. It was your brain following the rule-based principle that X = Y: the round shape and the sound fit on a conceptual level. This example comes from an experiment, conducted in 1933, by famous German psychologist Wolfgang Köhler. His results always showed the same effect: 'buba' was assigned to more rounded shapes, while 'kiki' was associated with the jagged shape.

As we grow up our brain learns something analogous to a set of statistics of our experiences and our environment – our 'environmental statistics'. In this way we bootstrap our associative memory using the learning rule of 'what fires together wires together'. The process by which we learn these patterns happens completely implicitly. Scott Kaufman at Yale University writes about this amazing ability in a summary published in the academic journal *Cognition* (2010):

> *The ability to automatically and implicitly recognize patterns and rules in our environment is a fundamental aspect of human cognition.*

As marketers we have the chance to ensure efficient communication by borrowing these implicit memories in order to associate our brand with the consumer goals with which we want it to be connected. It's very difficult to establish wholly new connections because, statistically, our marketing communication is only a tiny amount of a consumer's experiences and will not be sufficient to impact their 'environmental statistics'. That would be like trying to make consumers fundamentally relearn – how

Figure 6.15 Syoss product range borrows the prototype of a professional haircare product that is familiar from the hair salon

much effort would it take to convince the autopilot that a rose stands for fun and not for love?

A lesson in how borrowed memories can be used for successful innovations comes from the haircare brand Syoss. They launched a new product based on the proposition that the consumer is now able to get haircare products that are normally only available at the stylist for a reasonable price in the supermarket. The launch was a great success. Let's have a look at the packaging (see Figure 6.15).

The packaging design consists of diagnostic codes that are strongly associated with the concept of professional product ranges that people have witnessed and learned from their hair salon. It fits the prototypical design of professional products. The signals use a well-trodden path to the intended concept of 'professional care'. Since this goal-based proposition was highly relevant and unique, the launch was successful.

The opportunity to replace lengthy subjective debates with objective and strategic decisions becomes clearer if we have the mental concept (activated through signals) and the corresponding customer goal as a reference for evaluation. We are then – thanks to environmental statistics – faced with clear and objective principles for whether or not packaging, advertising or any other touchpoint conveys the intended goal, i.e. the strategy, better than its predecessor or its alternatives. What this shows is that the meaning of signals is not arbitrary or just subject to personal liking or taste. Can you recall conversations where people in the business have said things such as, 'I like the bit where she does XYZ but I don't like ABC' or 'I really like such and such design element but I don't like this colour'? But whether we like something or not is clearly not an objective way to judge signals. Liking is the wrong question. The key question is whether a signal prototypically stands for the intended value proposition in our culture. The key is the word *prototypical* because if we base our communication on weak associations between the signal and the proposition, then its effectiveness will suffer – especially if consumers process the message not reflectively but on autopilot.

Within a given culture we share the associations between signals, mental concepts and goals due to our shared socialization. Hence it is not arbitrary what concept a signal triggers. Environmental statistics offer clear and objective principles for whether or not signals address the intended goal.

Borrowed memories are culture specific

Since our memories are grounded in the culture in which we grow up and live, borrowed memories in our campaigns are also bound to be, at least in part, culture specific. The tendency in brand management is to have multinational campaigns that are highly similar or even identical across countries. The autopilot implicitly derives rules for the connection of signals and mental concepts from our daily experiences. This includes both the environment and the culture in which we grow up. Take a look at the well-known visual illusion in Figure 6.16. It seems that one line is longer than the other when in fact they are exactly the same length.

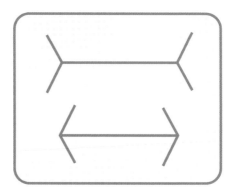

Figure 6.16 The famous Muller–Lyer illusion

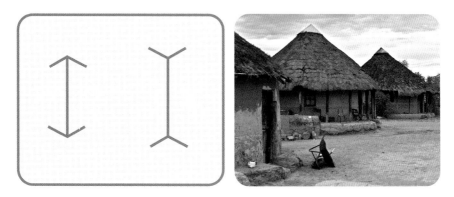

Figure 6.17 The environmental statistics shape how we perceive signals
Source: Shutterstock.com

What is interesting here is that South African Zulus do not fall for this illusion. Why not? They live in round huts, plough in curves and their belongings rarely have straight edges. Our rooms and houses, meanwhile, are angular. We therefore learn implicitly that depending on perspective, one configuration signifies 'close' and the other 'further away' (see Figure 6.17).

Understanding that the culture and environment in which we grow up play a determinative role in setting the rules by which our autopilots decode signals can liberate our decision making in everyday marketing. Those who grew up in a common country or culture all share the same environmental statistics. So we know the connections from that environment; they're there, learned implicitly, in our autopilot. Gaps will exist if we have had no access to a particular environment, such as youth culture or a foreign culture, because we did not learn the same X = Y connections as people subjected to those cultures. From this, there is a clear implication for multinational companies that judgement of whether signals connect to concepts should not be made by someone who lacks the environmental statistics for where the activity will take place.

It may well be that different signals are required in certain cultures in order to connect to the concept that the brand intends to communicate. There are many cases where signals have completely different associations. The chocolate brand Milka uses a cow on its packaging, for instance. While the connection between cow/milk and chocolate/goodness is obvious and perfectly acceptable in some cultures, it would not be possible to use the same signal in India where a cow is a sacred animal. Another case would be the use of the colour green, which is venerated in the Islamic culture. Cleanliness is coded by a different scent in the UK and Germany (citrus), than in Spain (chlorine).

This does not imply, though, that each and every country needs a different advertising execution as it is still possible to have international campaigns where there are sufficient commonalities between the environments. What's needed is some examination of where there are similarities in the relevant environmental statistics, i.e. whether the same connections between signals and concepts exist. There is a rule of thumb that can help to judge whether a signal may be understood differently or consistently across cultures: the more tangible the signal, the higher the probability that it has consistent meaning across cultures. So shapes and colours show less variability in meaning compared with scent. Scent is not tangible at all and hence is easily recoded into many things. This is why the US army has not been able to develop a stink bomb that works across the world, as even something basic like judging whether or not a scent is disgusting is culture specific. If signals are less tangible, such as scent, they can more easily be overruled by other signals. If we test the identical scent of a product in different bottles, with different colours or names, the scent will be perceived differently. (Remember the impact of the food colouring on the perceived taste of the food?)

So the approach of using environmental statistics and learning principles helps us to build a basis for objective evaluation and discussion within marketing and agencies. No matter how different we may be as people, we have all learned the same rules, at least those within our common culture. We have also all learned the same connections between signals and mental concepts. If we didn't know the same rules, it would be much more difficult to coexist. If any doubt remains, however, there is always the possibility of measuring the strength of association with an implicit priming test to prove whether a key visual, shape, story or testimonial triggers the intended concepts in the relevant markets. While local adaptations may be needed, the key strategic challenge is to ensure consistency in translating the value proposition. The brand should be consistent at the goal level, across both touchpoints and markets. Local adaptations or redesigns and new launches are effective only if they can convey the intended proposition better in a given market.

Signals can be used across cultures provided they trigger the same mental concept in the respective cultures.

Baked in – signals determine credibility

Being able to manage, and have discussions, with more objectivity provides for more efficient internal processes and more effective consumer communication. With an objective basis to judge any kind of communication, the third and final success factor besides relevance and differentiation can be achieved: credibility.

Our propositions and our executions need to be credible in order to be persuasive. In marketing we always ask if a message is credible, but a closer look reveals that there are different levels of credibility. The first level is based on the positive attitude and trust the consumer has in the brand in the sense of 'I believe what they tell me because it is a trusted brand'. This does not address the specific proposition or signals; it's more of an overall positive attitude. The second level is the logic of the argument. If the argument of the proposition is sufficiently intuitive, consumers rate a concept, for example, as being credible. But there is a third, more implicit level of credibility in the sense of 'is there any perceivable signal that makes the proposition tangible?'.

The case of Syoss hair products shows that using prototypical signals of professional haircare made the proposition tangible, and thus credible. Without a signal that tangibly proves the proposition, no mental concept is activated and hence no goal is addressed. It is then merely a claim, which is much less credible for the autopilot. This is one of the main obstacles for innovations: does any improvement result in a noticeably different product experience? Assume you currently have a camera with 5 mega-pixel resolution and you are offered a new camera with 5.5 megapixels. Would you expect to get a different experience? Would this improvement motivate you to buy? What if it were 6 megapixels? Or 8 megapixels? The question is how big does a difference – be it a product improvement or a price reduction – have to be to really perceivably change the value–cost relationship? Figure 6.18 shows the result of a measurement we did a while back on exactly this question.

We can see that a significant contrast in perceived value is reached only with a resolution of 7.5 megapixels, or, in other words, only with an improvement of 2.5 megapixels from our starting point of 5 megapixels. All the incremental steps in between can be dispensed with. To customers there is no recognisable difference whether the camera has three, four or five mega pixels – a difference is only recognised when we get to 7.5

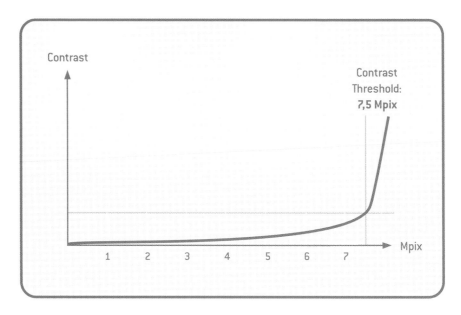

Figure 6.18 Just Noticeable Difference: when does the change make a difference?

megapixels. This is where the difference starts to be noticed. The term which is used in science for this critical difference is JND – Just Noticeable Difference. If we were to put our hand in a cup of water and the temperature of the water was gradually increased, we would not notice it until a point where it suddenly became too hot, since each prior increase was below the Just Noticeable Difference threshold.

This has far-reaching consequences for marketing. Let's take pricing. At what point does a price difference really make a difference? At what point does it exceed the JND? The goal must be to increase the price to just below the JND. The key question when it comes to product features is: at what point does an improvement really make a difference, thereby increasing the perceived value of the product by serving additional consumer goals or meeting existing goals better? Stabilo Boss, the pen manufacturer, worked on lengthening the 'cap-off' time – the number of hours which a marker pen can be left minus its cap without drying out – from

100 hours to 120 hours. But does this difference make a difference to the customer? Does it increase the perceived value?

If the improvement is not perceivable, if it does not make a difference in the tangible product experience, it hardly adds perceived value. This is one reason why many innovations fail. If we were able to gauge the JND of product improvements we would then be able to allocate our spending on innovation more effectively by focusing on those improvements that can, and will, be perceived as different. Sometimes the driver of improvements is somewhat artificial, i.e. to have some 'new news' to tell, but we should note that, for the autopilot, the only differences that matter are those that are perceptible and those that we can experience. We can accomplish innovation in saturated markets mainly by being different, and not by being better.

Pay TV illustrates this point well. Apart from exclusive content they face a hard time making tangible their claims of 'the better way to watch TV'. Consumers do the same things, the receivers mostly look like each other, and their usage is broadly the same. An example that makes the claimed uniqueness of the product experience tangible is 'Le Cube' from the French company Canal+. It obviously looks different, and using it is very different yet still ergonomical and intuitive (see Figure 6.19).

Coors Light, the beer brand, claims to offer 'Refreshment as cold as the Rockies'. This positioning is baked in to the packaging via the so-called Cold Activated Bottle (see Figure 6.20) – the mountains on the label turn blue when the beer has reached a certain temperature and thus signal cold, freshness and refreshment. Overall it is the packaging – not the beer itself – which is responsible for the credibility of the positioning since any beer will refresh when it's cold. The packaging, therefore, delivers a differentiating signal, which is directly coupled with the goal of 'refreshment'.

Credibility in this sense is not about explicitly believing in or trusting something but rather whether a consumer can experience and perceive

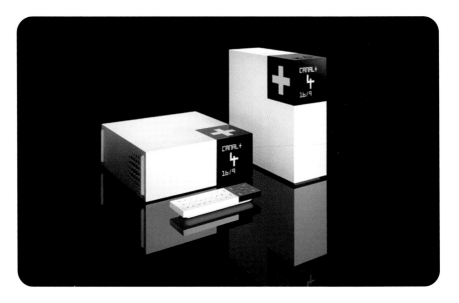

Figure 6.19 The 'Le Cube' receiver from Canal+ makes the different usage experience tangible

Figure 6.20 The Cold Activated Bottle adds perceivable differentiation and supports the refreshment proposition

Figure 6.21 Short Black delivers the prototypical diagnostic codes of espresso to credibly differentiate it from regular coffee

something through their senses. This Coors Light innovation is not an objective improvement but rather a symbolic innovation which uses a tangible signal to activate or strengthen a mental concept that connects to a relevant goal.

We have already argued that this new approach of using environmental statistics and guidelines from within the brain does not restrict creativity. Creativity is important but it must be credible. This is where the insight into environmental statistics helps, since this is where the foundation of our everyday experience lies – and this is the only source of credibility. A good example of where environmental statistics can help is the Short Black espresso from Nescafé Australia (see Figure 6.21). What is portrayed here are the key attributes that distinguish espresso from regular coffee.

According to environmental statistics, espresso is short and strong ('the short one'). The packaging signals convey exactly what we want from an espresso by using black as a colour and taking 'short' literally (though

A value proposition is credible if the product experience provides tangible signals so that the proposition can be experienced.

there may be issues with volume perception due to the reduction in height, which may bias consumers to underestimate the number of servings contained).

The bottom-up approach to credible propositions

As marketers we have two options to derive credible propositions: we can create a product experience consisting of tangible signals based on a goal-based value proposition (top-down approach), or we can identify the mental concepts that are baked in to the product experience and build the goal-based proposition upon it (bottom-up approach). Both routes ensure credibility.

We have focused so far on the top-down approach. However, we often face the case where we already have a product and our task is to develop a unique, differentiating and credible proposition for it, i.e. we have to work bottom-up from the product. Imagine we have to create a value proposition for an instant coffee. To do so, we have to look at the tangible product experience and to which goals it is connected. In order to achieve uniqueness we have to compare it against our main competitor: roasted coffee. Our autopilot gets input from all our senses, so let's go through the senses since they determine the product experience.

First of all, the product looks different. Both are brown, but the instant one is less saturated in colour, less full-bodied and less dark. These characteristics have direct mental equivalents. This is a first clue for the expectation that ground coffee tastes different, fuller-bodied and richer, which fits with its more intensive aroma. Second, the haptic (touching) experience is different. The instant coffee is granular, hard and angular and the roasted coffee feels soft and smooth like fine sand (see Figure 6.22). Besides the sensory experience, the way we brew and serve it is also

Figure 6.22 Differences in product experience link the two products to different goals

different. Roasted coffee is prepared in a pot and everyone gets the same coffee whereas with instant coffee everyone gets coffee prepared individually in their own cup.

Core goals achieved through serving coffee are harmony and getting together, which are both located in the security territory. So looking at the category it would be a good idea to link the instant coffee product to this goal. However, this would not be credible because the product experience is more strongly connected with individuality. No one would serve instant coffee at a formal family gathering. Therefore the linkage between instant coffee and harmony would not be credible because it is not baked in to the product experience and therefore not baked into the product.

Deconstructing the product experience into its perceivable entities provides a powerful springboard for developing relevant, unique and credible value propositions.

When looking at the product experience we sometimes undervalue the specifics that are experienced during the actual process of usage or

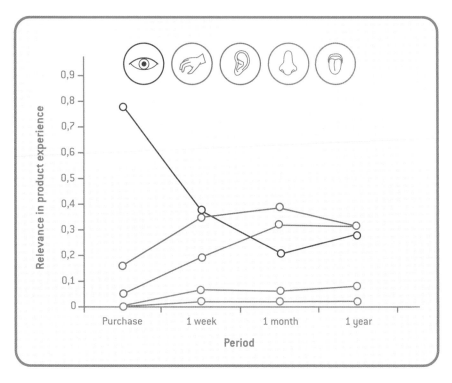

Figure 6.23 The influence of the senses varies along the usage process

consumption. Figure 6.23 shows that the senses provide opportunities, as well as potential barriers, for credibility.

At the point of purchase the visual experience is crucial. However, the other senses should not be neglected since they constitute the entirety of the product experience so they are important triggers for credibility of the proposition and its implementation. In addition, looking at the total usage experience is crucial for spotting opportunities for differentiation and relevance.

Embodied cognition – our body thinks as well

So far we have looked at how the input from our senses, especially the visual sense, contributes to credibility. In the case of instant coffee we have

Figure 6.24 Does the way the deodorant is opened fit with masculinity?

already taken consumer behaviour, the handling of the product, into account. The fascinating field of embodied cognition shows that what we do and how we do things, e.g. how we open a pack or how we prepare coffee or how we use the product, also activates mental concepts. In a way our body is a sixth sense in which meaning is also baked in.

Let's look at an example. Figure 6.24 shows the cap of a deodorant aerosol. This deodorant is designed especially for men. It is silver, and the packaging contains words such as 'power' and 'dynamic', which are the mental concepts that the product wants to address. Neuropsychologists have researched the concepts with which hand grips are principally connected.

Figure 6.25 shows prototypical grips, what they signify and what they transmit to the autopilot. The first distinction is between power grips and fine grips. In the case of the deodorant the cap is opened with a fine grip, which is not prototypically associated with masculinity, power or dynamism. In order for packaging to convey a male concept, a power grip is required. As such, this packaging characteristic is wrong for a male deodorant.

Scientists from the American National Institute of Mental Health showed a picture of a cup to study participants who were being monitored in a

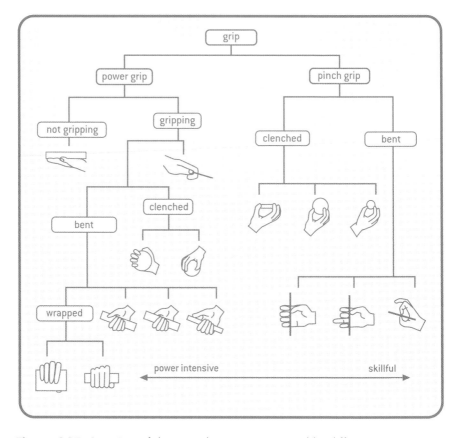

Figure 6.25 Overview of the mental concepts conveyed by different grips

brain scanner. As expected, this activated the visual cortex, i.e. that part of the brain responsible for processing visual signals. The surprising thing, however, was that the motor cortex, too, reacted to the sight of the cup. To explain, the motor cortex is the part of our brain that is responsible for the movement of our arms and legs. The researchers followed up this phenomenon by showing the study participants pictures of different cups as well as an image containing only the word 'cup'. All of these images also activated the part of the brain responsible for handling a cup. The mere sight of a cup or even the word 'cup' causes the same neural response as if we were actually holding one.

So whenever we look at a product, the areas within the brain which are relevant to handling the product are activated – from sight to gripping, opening or pushing with our hands. Understanding is linked closely to handling in the brain. To answer the question 'what is it?', our brain simulates how we would hold, handle and use it – we simulate what we can do with it. This process, again, takes place automatically and entirely implicitly – we do not consciously perceive it. Scientists refer to this as 'embodied cognition'.

Mental concepts and goals can be activated not only through the senses but also through embodiment: what we do with products and how we handle them.

Let's have a look at the iPhone with this perspective in mind (see Figure 6.26). Technologically the iPhone is not superior to most of the other smartphones – any relevant explicit goals can be met with them all. Beside the fact that it is an Apple product (which adds implicit goals such as creativity, sophistication and exclusivity), the main difference when it was launched was the way in which it was operated – its touchscreen and its operation by finger. Embodied cognition indicates that there is more to this than just convenience or intuitive handling since using thumbs when operating a Blackberry device is also intuitive. So which mental concept is activated by interacting with the iPhone?

Suggestion

Before you continue reading, take a closer look at the finger movements in the images. Copy them and ask yourself the following questions: 'When do I prototypically use these finger movements?' 'In which other situations do I do/have I done something like this?'

The first typical finger movement in operating the iPhone is a kind of flicking – the movement of our index finger is as we might, for example, flick cards across a table. At least that's how most iPhone users 'turn pages'. What kind of flicking is this? What else is flicked like this, where

Figure 6.26 Apple's iPhone triggers a mental concept

does our associative memory know this from? Let's look again at this finger movement. Is it more like leafing through a book or a magazine? Most people associate the turning of thinner, lighter and more flexible pages with it. When turning heavier pages, we tend to use the thumb as well; therefore, it must be more like a magazine. This activates everything we know about a magazine, the occasions on which we read a magazine and which goals are active when we read a magazine. When do we read 'Heat' magazine or 'OK' and why? Reading a magazine is highly associated with leisure and distraction. Which connections relate to the finger movements when operating an iPhone? Concentrated working? No, it's much more about 'relaxation' and 'entertainment'. It may happen implicitly, without us realizing, but we have already seen that something as simple as perceiving a product with the eye involves many different steps in the autopilot, none of which we are aware of.

The second typical action when using an iPhone is scrolling with the index finger. The index finger is put onto the touchscreen and then pulled back. After a short distance, the index finger is retracted and slightly removed from the touchscreen. Which mental concept is activated through this action? In order to unlock the code we must ask ourselves the same question as the autopilot in our head: 'Where do I know this from?' We need to find the prototypical things which we associate with this movement. We usually make this type of finger movement when we turn something, for instance a small wheel. The way in which we turn these further shows us that the wheel turns or spins slightly further than we intended (as does the iPhone). If we want to control where the wheel stops, we don't retract the index finger as far, as we want to be able to stop it quickly – we let the wheel run a bit and are not entirely sure where it will stop. Implicitly, therefore, this contains an element of surprise, much like when we play a fruit machine. Observing children, we can see that this movement is carried out by playing with a wheel, perhaps on a toy car – to start with, they may use their whole hand and then only the index finger; therefore, the concepts of 'play' and 'surprise' are activated connectively.

A further prototypical way of using the iPhone is tapping with the fingertip. The finger is either slightly lifted or slightly bent in order to touch the particular area of the touchscreen that we want to activate. When else do we do this? From where does our brain recognize this action? We do this when we point to something, indicate a direction or turn something on. We also do this when we use a computer's mouse. Both are coupled with direction or activation. When we click through to a link on the internet, we either want to access a page or we want to activate something. 'Direction' and 'activation' are therefore also activated implicitly. On top of all of its technical functionality, the iPhone operation is a code for relaxation, light entertainment, playing, surprise, activation and direction. No wonder that Apple patented the underlying gestures – they are crucial drivers for its success. If we observe iPhone users, we can see precisely these operating movements. It is about playing – not working.

The Blackberry, meanwhile, is operated by thumb. When do we use our thumbs? When we need strength and want to turn something in a controlled or precise fashion, like a dial or a combination lock. 'Control' and 'work' are the overriding concepts here. As in the case of sensory signals such as shapes or colours, we can use implicit testing to objectively measure the concepts triggered by interacting with a product such as the iPhone and the Blackberry. Figure 6.27 shows the strongest associations triggered when handling both devices. The result is not surprising as we have seen that the meaning of signals and actions is not arbitrary but

leisure, play, surprise, activation, direction

work, control, stability

Figure 6.27 The two different product experiences address different goals

250

rather depends on our daily experience and the corresponding traces in associative memory.

Against this background, the usage demonstration of the iPhone in their adverts is not only a creative idea, it also brings the actual differentiating product code into focus. The adverts show the finger movements and thereby instantly activate the mental concepts that are associated with the product. By changing the way phones were handled, the iPhone introduced new goals in the smartphone market so it represented not only a technological innovation but also a so-called symbolic innovation. It owns these goals and they help to differentiate the iPhone brand from the competition.

What we have learned in this chapter

- We can close the implementation gap by, first, basing our strategy on the relevant and differentiating consumer goals and, second, using this strategy as the guiding principle to create product experiences and communication, and also to judge whether an execution credibly fits the strategy.
- The concept of emotions is too vague to guide implementation. Emotions are also too generic to enable relevant differentiation in a market.
- Value propositions are credible if the entire product experience delivers tangible signals that bridge to the addressed goals.

What this means to us as marketers

- A goal-based strategy provides clear guidance for implementation across all touchpoints. The implicit goal level in particular provides the opportunity to translate the value proposition in a creative, relevant and differentiating way.
- Once the strategy is goal based, the executional evaluation changes from 'do we like it?' to 'does it fit to the strategy?' Based on borrowed memory and environmental statistics, the latter question can be answered objectively.
- Deconstruction of the product experience into its perceivable entities provides a powerful springboard for developing relevant, unique and credible value propositions.

Closing Remarks

We have now come to the end of our journey. I started this book by saying that I'd been confronted with a fascinating and new mental model for marketing and consumer decision making, based on the latest scientific findings in the area of decision science. By now I'm sure that you share my view that we can now understand much previously unexplained consumer behaviour.

There are those in marketing who may have already suspected, or even have known, some of the findings contained herein, but the key thing is that we now have a more analytical, evidence-based framework to access consumer decision making. The core insight behind this is the importance of the implicit level of decision making. Integrating this implicit level into our day-to-day marketing practice results in a paradigm shift, giving us an entirely new perspective from which we can manage our products, services and brands. This new perspective offers us a great opportunity to generate superior net value for our customers, and hence to significantly increase our sales. It also helps us to close the implementation gap between strategy and execution and, in doing so, substantially reduces the risk of failure of new product developments and relaunches, and also makes our advertising budgets more effective.

This book also started with a major challenge to marketers: a study showing that CEOs do not think highly of marketing, in large part because of its intangibility – referring to it as 'la la land'. This book has shown that there is an alternative – a tangible, objective, science-based approach to marketing –that offers a way out of 'la la land' and into a position of greater understanding and respect in the boardroom.

Now you will understand why I was motivated to make the changes I did, both as the T-Mobile brand custodian and subsequently in changing careers. In my view, it's a no-brainer to adopt this approach to brand management – if you don't, then what if your competitors do? I sincerely hope that I've given you sufficient reason, enthusiasm and determination to make it happen in your business.

If you want to keep up with the latest insights from the fields of behavioural economics, psychology and neuroscience, sign up to our regular Science Updates at our website: www.decoded-book.com.

Acknowledgements

This book would never have come into being had it not been for the 'decision scientists' from decode in the first place. Thank you for lifting the veil on how human beings really work. Also, for answering each and every question that this marketer could throw at you. I've lost count of the number of 'aha' moments I've had since we met!

In particular I would like to thank my colleagues Dr Christian Scheier, Dirk Held and Steve Baily for their awesome contributions. This book has flourished and blossomed thanks to their continued efforts and expertise.

Thanks, too, go to Annette Gräf for the illustrations, to Michaela Fay from John Wiley & Sons for being gentle with a virgin author, to Lainey for her love and support, to Mark Earls, Wendy Gordon, Sean Gogarty, Phil Chapman, Chris Barrow, Paul Fishlock, Philip Graves, Margaret Johnson and Professors Barwise, Camerer and Zurawicki for their enthusiastic advocacy and citations, and finally, to the bounteous Rory Sutherland for lending his considerable intellect and tireless enthusiasm to the new order of consumer understanding. I'm honoured that he has written the foreword.

Recommended Reading

Ariely, D. and Norton, M.I. (2009). How concepts affect consumption. *Annual Review of Psychology*, 60, 475–499. Summary of the concepts affecting consumption by well-known behavioural economist Dan Ariely.

Bazerman, M.H. (2006). *Judgment in Managerial Decision Making*. Hoboken, NJ: John Wiley & Sons, Inc. In this major work Harvard Professor Bazerman describes what effects the implicit system has on the decision-making behaviour of managers.

Hassin, R.R., Uleman, J.S. and Bargh, J.A. (2005). *The New Unconscious*. Oxford: Oxford University Press. Comprehensive review of research into the new unconscious. Aimed at those more interested in the science.

Kahneman, D. (2011). *Thinking, Fast and Slow*. New York: Macmillan. The bestselling introduction to the world of the autopilot (system 1) and the pilot (system 2) by Nobel Prize laureate Daniel Kahneman.

Lieberman, M.D. (2007). Social cognitive neuroscience: A review of core processes. *Annual Review of Psychology*, 58, 259–289. Sound overview of the neural basis of the autopilot and the pilot.

Moskowitz, G. and Grant, H. (ed.) (2009). *The Psychology of Goals*. New York: The Guilford Press. Current reference work on the psychology of goals. Shows very clearly the connection of goals with signals and the integration of motivation and cognition in the brain. Also shows that goals are regulated implicitly, and how.

Ratneshwar, S. *et al.* (ed.) (2000). *The Why of Consumption. Contemporary perspectives on consumer motives, goals and desires*. London and New York: Routledge. Gives a good overview of the science of consumer goals.

Sommer, S. (2011). *Situations Matter: Understanding How Context Transforms Your World*. New York: Riverhead Hardcover. Written by a social psychologist, this book shows how situations and context shape our decisions.

Thaler, R.H. and Sunstein, C.R. (2009). *Nudge: Improving Decisions about Health, Wealth, and Happiness*. London: Penguin. Standard reference work on the application of behavioural economics in society and politics.

Wilson, T.D. (2004). *Strangers to Ourselves: Discovering the Adaptive Unconscious*. Cambridge: Harvard University Press. A highly readable introduction to the science of the autopilot with many references and further scientific studies on the 'new unconscious'.

Further reading suggestions and literature referenced in the book

Ackermann, J.M., Nocera, C.C. and Bargh, J.A. (2010). Incidental haptic sensations influence social judgments and decisions. *Science*, 328, 1712–1715. Article showing the interaction of haptic perception with cognitive processing, and the implications for our decisions and our behaviour.

Allcott, H. (2011). Social norms and energy conservation. *Journal of Public Economics*. 95 (9–10), 1082–1095.

Arana, F.S., Parkinson, A., Hinton, E., Holland, A.J., Owen A.M. and Roberts, A.C. (2003). Dissociable contributions of the human amygdala and orbitofrontal cortex to incentive motivation and goal selection. *Journal of Neuroscience*, 23 (29), S. 9632–9638. Shows the central role of the orbito-frontal cortex in decision making.

Ariely, D. (2010). *Predictably Irrational: The hidden forces that shape our decisions*. HarperCollins. A well-written introduction to the implicit influences on our behaviour by one of the leading behavioural economists.

Atlas, L.Y., and Wager, T.D. (2012). How expectations shape pain. Neuroscience Letters 520(2), 140–148.

Bar, M. (2004). Visual objects in context. *Nature Reviews: Neuroscience*, 5, 617–629. Shows that object recognition is heavily influenced by contextual information.

Barrett, L.F. and Bar, M. (2009). See it with feeling: affective predictions during object perception. Philosophical Transactions of the Royal Society B. 364, 1325–1334. Shows that perception is heavily influenced by valuation.

Berns, G.S. and Moore, S.E. (2012). A neural predictor of cultural popularity. *Journal of Consumer Psychology*, 22 (1), 154–160. Shows that activity in the reward centre in the brain is correlated with purchases even on a population level.

Berridge, K.C. and Robinson, T.E. (2003). Parsing reward. *Trends in Neurosciences*, 26 (9), 507–513. Good overview of the neurobiological and psychological reward systems.

Christensen, C.M., Cook, S. and Hall, T. (2009). Marketing malpractice: the cause and the cure. *Harvard Business Review*, 83 (12), 74–83. Brilliant article about the role of consumer goals for segmentation, new product development and marketing in general.

Cialdini, R.B. (2006). *Influence: The Psychology of Persuasion*. HarperBusiness. The bestselling book by American social psychologist and consultant Robert Cialdini shows how the autopilot is noticeable in everyday life.

Coulter, Keith S., and Patricia Norberg, (2009) The effects of physical distance between regular and sale prices on numeric difference perceptions. *Journal of Consumer Psychology*. Conditionally accepted for publication (with minor revisions) September 1, 2008.

Cunningham W.A. *et al.* (2011). Orbitofrontal cortex provides cross-modal valuation of self-generated stimuli. *Social Cognitive and Affective Neuroscience*, 6 (4) 460–467. Exciting study that provides evidence that the frontal lobe assesses not only real products but also mental concepts for their relevance. Also confirms the finding that the brain uses a common currency, that of 'wanting to have'.

Custers, R. and Aarts, H. (2010). The unconscious will: how the pursuit of goals operates outside of conscious awareness. *Science*, 329, 47–50. Accounts of various experiments that show behaviour is regulated by implicit goals.

de Araujo, I.E., Rolls, E.T., Velazco, M.I., Margot, C. and Cayeux, I. (2005). Cognitive modulation of olfactory processing. *Neuron*, 46 (4), 671–679. Verbal labels change the subjective pleasantness and neuronal activation of scents.

De Martino, B. *et al.* (2009). The neurobiology of reference-dependent value computation. *Journal of Neuroscience*, 29 (12), 3833–3842. Shows that willingness to pay depends on the implicit context.

Degonda, N., Mondadori, C.R.A., Bosshardt, S., Schmidt, C.F., Boesiger, P., Nitsch, R., Hock, C. and Henke Westerholt, K. (2005). Implicit associative learning engages the hippocampus and interactions with explicit associative learning. *Neuron*, 46, S. 505–520. Article defining the foundation of cultural implicit learning processes in the hippocampus and their influence on conscious learning.

Deppe, M., Schwindt, W., Krämer, J., Kugel, H., Plassmann, H., Kenning, P. and Ringelstein, E.B. (2005). Evidence for a neural correlate of a framing effect: bias-specific activity in the ventromedial prefrontal cortex during credibility judgments. *Brain Research Bulletin*, 67, S. 413–421. Focuses on the framing effect for media brands at the neuronal level.

Dijksterhuis, A. and Arts, H. (2010). Goals, attention, and (un)consciousness. *Annual Review of Psychology*, 61, 467–490. Very good insight and overview of the finding that our goals are implicitly regulated and that attention and consciousness in the brain are two separate things.

Dijksterhuis, A., Maarten, W.B., Nordgren, L.F. and van Baaren, R.B. (2006). On making the right choice: the deliberation-without-attention-effect. *Science*, 311, S. 1005. Shows that (and how) thinking often results in worse decisions compared with intuitive, 'autopilot' decisions – even in complex decisions.

Duhigg, C. (2012). *The Power of Habit: Why We Do What We Do in Life and Business*. New York: Random House. Excellent introduction to the power of habits.

Earls, M. (2007). *Herd? – How to Change Mass Behaviour by Harnessing Our True Nature*. West Sussex: John Wiley & Sons Ltd. Former planner Mark Earls received an award for his article in which he attacks the individualistic view of marketing and stresses the social nature of man. This book, a great read, arose from that article.

Elder, R.S. and Krishna, A. (2011). The 'visual depiction effect' in advertising: facilitating embodied mental simulation through product orientation. *Journal of Consumer Research*, 38, 1–17. The way products are shown in ads greatly influences persuasion through embodied mental simulations.

Ferguson, M.J. and Porter, S.C. (2010). What is implicit about goal pursuit? B. Gawronski and K. Payne (Eds.), Handbook of Implicit Social Cognition. Guilford Press.

Fitzsimons, G., Hutchinson, J.W. and Williams, P. (2002). Non-conscious influences on consumer choice. *Marketing Letters*, 13, S. 269–279. Excellent introduction and overview on implicit influences on consumer purchase behaviour.

Franzen, G. and Bouwman, M. (2001). *The Mental World of Brands*. Trowbridge: Cromwell Press. A thorough introduction to the world of brands in neural networks.

Gallese, V. and Lakoff, G. (2005). The brain's concepts: The role of the sensory-motor system in conceptual knowledge. *Cognitive Neuropsychology*, 22 (3/4) 455–479. A linguist and a neuroscientist, both top experts in their fields, put together the relevant findings from 'embodied cognition' to explain how the body structures our mental world.

GfK (Gesellschaft für Konsumforschung) (2007). Typology of watch purchases. Report by GfK (in German).

Gigerenzer, G. (2008). *Gut Feelings: The Intelligence of the Unconscious*. London and New York: Penguin Books. Excellent overview on how intuition works and helps in decision making.

Gigerenzer, G., Todd P.M. and ABC Research Group (2000). *Simple Heuristics That Make Us Smart*. New York: Oxford University Press. Provides a deep dive into the world of heuristics.

Gosling, S.D., Ko, S.J., Mannarelli, T. and Morris, M.E. (2002). A room with a cue: judgments of personality based on offices and bedrooms. *Journal of Personality and Social Psychology*, 82, 379–398. Our autopilot easily decodes the personalities of people simply from pictures of their homes.

Graves, P. (2011). *Consumer-ology: The Market Research Myth, the Truth about Consumers and the Psychology of Shopping*. Boston and London: Nicholas Brealey. Illustrates the implications for market research of the implicit decision-making level.

Hanks, A.S., Just, D.R., Smith, L.E. and Wansink, B. (2012). Healthy convenience: nudging students toward healthier choices in the lunchroom, *Journal of Public Health*, 34 (3) 370–376. Describes the canteen experiment (at the beginning of Chapter 4) and shows how changes to the decision interface influence decision making.

Hare T.A. *et al.* (2008). Dissociating the role of the orbitofrontal cortex and the striatum in the computation of goal values and prediction. *Journal of Neuroscience*, 28, 5623–5630. Shows the frontal lobe's neural basis for the assessment of target value (goal value) and its importance in making decisions.

Harrell PT, and Juliano LM (2009). Caffeine expectancies influence the subjective and behavioral effects of caffeine. Psychopharmacology.

Heath, R. (2012). *Seducing the Subconscious: The Psychology of Emotional Influence in Advertising*. Hoboken, NJ: Wiley-Blackwell. Provides an in-depth overview of implicit advertising effects, including implicit learning and peripheral perception.

Helbig, H. *et al.* (2010). Action observation can prime visual object recognition. *Experimental Brain Research*, 200, 251–258. Shows how gestures help in the identification of objects.

Irmak, C. *et al.* (2005). The placebo effect in marketing: sometimes you just have to want it to work. *Journal of Marketing Research*, 42, 406–409. Shows the placebo effect of an energy drink in increasing blood pressure.

Isanski, B. and West, C. (2010). The body of knowledge. Understanding embodied cognition. *Observer*, 23 (1). Very good and clear summary of the current knowledge on 'embodied cognition' from the journal Observer of the Association for Psychological Science.

Kahneman, D. (2002). Maps of bounded rationality. http://nobelprize.org/nobel_prizes/economics/laureates/2002/kahneman-lecture.html. The Nobel Prize acceptance speech by Daniel Kahneman, to which we refer in the first part of this book. The web link offers a video of this exciting presentation.

Kahneman, D. and Frederick, S. (2002). Representativeness revisited: Attribute substitution in intuitive judgment. In: Gilovich, T., Griffin, D. and Kahneman, D. (eds.) *Heuristics and Biases: The Psychology of Intuitive Judgment*. New York: Cambridge University Press. S. 67–83. Classic paper by Daniel Kahneman showing how (product) attributes are being used in intuitive decision making.

Kaufman, S.B. *et al.* (2010). Implicit learning as an ability. *Cognition*, 116 (3) 321–340. Shows how the brain learns, through implicit learning of environmental statistics, and how this implicit learning corresponds with intelligence.

Knutson, B., Rick, S., Wimmer, E., Prelec, D. and Loewenstein, G. (2007). Neural predictors of purchases. *Neuron*, 53, 147–156. Shows that the reward system is activated when viewing products and brands whereas, in contrast, price activates the pain centre.

Levin, I.P., Schreiber, J., Lauriola, M. and Gaeth, G.J. (2002). A tale of two pizzas: building up from a basic product versus scaling down from a fully-loaded product. *Marketing Letters*, 13 (4), 335–344.

Li, W., Luxenberg, E., Parrish, T., and Gottfried, J.A. (2006). Learning to smell the roses: experience-dependent neural plasticity in human piriform and orbitofrontal cortices. Neuron 52: 1097–1108.

Martin, A. (2007). The representation of object concepts in the brain. *Annual Review of Psychology*, 58, 25–45. Very well-founded overview of how the brain organizes mental concepts.

Martin, N. (2008). *Habit: The 95 Per Cent of Behavior Marketers Ignore*. New Jersey: FT Press. Overview of the power of habits and how to use them to good effect in marketing.

McClure, S.M., Li, J., Tomlin, D., Cypert, K.S., Montague, L.M. and Montague, P.R. (2004). Neural correlates of behavioral preference for culturally familiar drinks. *Neuron*, 44, S. 379–387. Classic neuro-economic study replicating the blind test of Coca-Cola vs. Pepsi in the brain scanner.

Meyers-Levy, J. and Maheswaran, D. (1990). Message framing effects on product judgments. Advances in Consumer Research, 17, 531–534.

Moerman, D. (2009). *Meaning, Medicine, and the 'Placebo Effect'*. Cambridge: Cambridge University Press. This highly recommended book demonstrates, clearly and concisely, the subtle and powerful effects of codes in medicine, including the placebo effect of aspirin packaging.

Morwitz, V.G., Steckel, J. and Gupta, A. (2007). When do purchase intentions predict sales? *International Journal of Forecasting*, 23 (3), 347–364.

Novemsky, N. *et al.* (2007). The effect of preference fluency on consumer decision making. *Journal of Marketing Research*, 19, 347–356. The authors show that the legibility of a font affects the purchasing decision.

Nunes, J.C. and Drèze, X. (2006). The endowed progress effect: how artificial advancement increases effort. *Journal of Consumer Research*, 32, 504–512. Investigates the effect that we are much more likely to complete a process if that process has already been started (the car wash example in Chapter 4).

Pieters, R. and Wedel, M. (2012). Ad gist: ad communication in a single eye fixation. *Marketing Science*, 59–73. Shows that in some ads, brand and product can be recognized in as little as 100 milliseconds – even when the ad is blurred.

Plassmann, H. *et al.* (2007). Orbitofrontal cortex encodes willingness to pay in everyday economic transactions. *Journal of Neuroscience*, 27 (37), 9984–9988. Neuroscientific experiments, showing that the willingness to pay is regulated in the frontal lobe.

Plassmann, H., O'Doherty, J., Shiv, B. and Rangel, A. (2008). Marketing actions can modulate neural representations of experienced pleasantness. Proceedings of the National Academy of Sciences (USA), 105 (3), 1050–1054. Shows that prices influence neuronal activation of the reward centre, for example the same wine triggers higher activation when framed with a higher price.

Quiroga, Q.R., Reddy, L., Kreiman, G., Koch, C. and Fried, I. (2005). Invariant visual representation by single neurons in the human brain. *Nature*, 435, S. 1102–1107. Shows that (and how) the brain decodes meaning (in this case Halle Berry) irrespective of how it is presented (written form, visual, etc.).

Raghubir, P. and Krishna, A. (1999). Vital dimensions in volume perception: can the eye fool the stomach? *Journal of Marketing Research*, 26 (3), 313–326. Investigates the fact that consumers judge volume based on the elongation of a package.

Rajagopal, R., Walker, R. and Hoyer, W. (2006). The 'unhealthy = tasty' intuition and its effects on taste inferences, enjoyment, and choice of food products, *Journal of Marketing*, 70 (4), 170–184. Uses an implicit measurement technique to show that people employ an implicit rule 'unhealthy = tasty' and that this is widely reflected in their behaviour.

Rolls, E.T. (2006). *Emotions Explained*. Oxford: Oxford University Press. Edmund T. Rolls is one of the leading neuroscientists and his speciality is the reward system in the brain, especially the orbitofrontal cortex. The book is aimed at those with a scientific interest and gives a thorough and comprehensive overview of what drives us: the pursuit of rewards.

Romaniuk, J. and Sharp, Byron. (2004). Conceptualizing and measuring brand salience. Marketing Theory, vol. 4, no. 4, pp. 327–342.

Schaefer, M. and Rotte, M. (2007). Favourite brands as cultural objects modulate reward circuit. *Neuroreport*, 18 (2), 141–145. These experiments show that brands activate the reward centre in the brain, and how they do this.

Schnall, S., Benton, J. and Harvey, S. (2008). With a clean conscience: cleanliness reduces the severity of moral judgments. *Psychological Science*, 19, 1219–1222. Shows the interaction between physical and moral cleanliness.

Seymour, B. and McClure, S.M. (2008). Anchors, scales and the relative coding of value in the brain. *Current Opinion in Neurobiology*, 18, 1–6. Discusses the relativity of value from a neuroscience perspective.

Shapiro, S. (1999). When an ad's influence is beyond our conscious control: perceptual and conceptual fluency effects caused by incidental ad exposure, *Journal of Consumer Research*, 26 (June), S. 16–36. Shows that ads can influence decisions even when processed by the autopilot.

Song, H. and Schwarz, N. (2008). If it's hard to read, it's hard to do. Processing fluency affects effort prediction and motivation. *Psychological Science*, 19, 986–988. Shows the effect of typography on cognition.

Stoll, M., Baecke, S. and Kenning, P. (2008). What they see is what they get? An fMRI-Study on neural correlates of attractive packaging. *Journal of Consumer Behaviour*, 7, 342–359. A neuroscientific study showing the neural effects of attractive packaging.

Strahan, E.J., Spencer, S.J. and Zanna, M.P. (2002). Subliminal priming and persuasion: striking while the iron is hot. *Journal of Experimental Social Psychology*, 38, S. 556–568. Shows that subliminal priming works if, and only if, there is a goal activated in the consumer mind that matches the subliminal stimulation.

Sutherland, R. (2011). *The Wiki Man*. London: Ogilvy Digital Labs. An introduction to the thinking and ideas of one of the leading marketing figures. Includes a liberal dose of behavioural economics insights.

Tanner, R.J. and Maeng, A. (in press). A tiger and a president: imperceptible celebrity facial cues influence trust and preference. *Journal of Consumer Research*, December. Shows the subtle yet powerful influence of faces in advertising.

Todorovic, A., van Ede, F., Maris, E. and de Lange, F.P. (2011). Prior expectation mediates neural adaptation to repeated sounds in the auditory cortex: an MEG study. *Journal of Neuroscience*, 31, 9118–9123.

Tusche, A., Bode, S. and Haynes, J.D. (2010). Neural responses to unattended products predict later consumer choices. *Journal of Neuroscience*, 30 (23), 8024–8031. Consumer choices could be predicted equally well in a low-attention group as they can in a high-attention group. This suggests that neural evaluation of products and associated choice-related processing does not necessarily depend on attentional processing of available stimuli. Overall, the present findings emphasize the potential of implicit, automatic processes in guiding even important and complex decisions.

Van Rompay, T.J.L., Pruyn, A.T.H. and Tieke, P. (2009). Symbolic meaning integration in design and its influence on product and brand evaluation. *International Journal of Design*, 3 (2), 19–26.

Vogt, J., De Houwer, J., Moors, A., Van Damme, S. and Crombez, G. (2010). The automatic orienting of attention to goal-relevant stimuli. *Acta Psychologica*, 134 (1), 61–69. Shows that attention is based on goal-relevance, and how.

Wansink, B. (2006). *Mindless Eating: Why We Eat More Than We Think*. New York: Bantam–Dell. Brilliant overview of the influence of implicit processing on the consumption of food by one of the leading researchers in this field.

Wansink, B., van Itterrsum, K. and Painter, J.M. (2005). How descriptive food names bias sensory perceptions in restaurants. *Food Quality and Preference*, 16 (5), 393–400. Shows how verbal labels can frame and influence the perceived quality of food.

Wedel, M. and Pieters, R. (2007). Goal control of attention to advertising: the Yarbus implication. *Journal of Consumer Research*, 34, 224–233. Highly recommended article that shows the influence of goals on the processing of advertising.

Williams, L.E. and Bargh, J.A. (2008). Experiencing physical warmth promotes interpersonal warmth. *Science*, 322, 606–607. Shows the effect of temperature on mental concepts.

Yang, S., Kimes, S.E. and Sessarego, S.S. (2009) Menu price presentation influences on consumer purchase behavior in restaurants. International Journal of Hospitality Management, 28 (1), 157–160.

Yarbus, Alfred L. (1967), Eye Movements and Vision, New York: Plenum Press.

Yoon, C. *et al.* (2006). A functional magnetic resonance imaging study of neural dissociations between brand and person judgments. *Journal of Consumer Research*, 33, 31–40. Shows, in a neuroscience experiment, that, in the brain, brands are not seen as people but as objects.

Zhong, C.B. and Leonardelli, G.J. (2008). Cold and lonely: does social exclusion literally feel cold? *Psychological Science*, 19, 838–842. The experiment, from Chapter 5, showing the link between social exclusion and the consequent desire for a hot soup or hot coffee.

Index